Libra

24 September – 23 October

First published in Great Britain 2009
by Harlequin Mills & Boon Limited,
Eton House, 18-24 Paradise Road, Richmond, Surrey TW9 1SR

ISBN: 978 0 263 87070 1

Typeset at Midland Typesetters Australia

Harlequin Mills & Boon policy is to use papers that are
natural, renewable and recyclable products and made from
wood grown in sustainable forests. The logging and
manufacturing processes conform to the legal environmental
regulations of the country of origin.

Printed and bound in Spain
by Litografia Rosés S.A., Barcelona

About
Dadhichi

Dadhichi is one of Australia's foremost astrologers. He has the ability to draw from complex astrological theory to provide clear, easily understandable advice and insights for people who want to know what their future might hold.

In the 26 years that Dadhichi has been practising astrology, face reading and other esoteric studies, he has conducted over 9,500 consultations. His clients include celebrities, political and diplomatic figures, and media and corporate identities from all over the world.

Dadhichi's unique blend of astrology and face reading helps people fulfil their true potential. His extensive experience practising western astrology is complemented by his research into the theory and practice of eastern systems of astrology.

Dadhichi features in numerous newspapers and magazines and he also appears regularly on many of Australia's leading television and radio networks, where many of his political and worldwide forecasts have proved uncannily accurate.

His website www.astrology.com.au is now one of the top ten online Australian lifestyle sites and, in conjunction with www.facereader.com, www.soulconnector.com and www.psychjuice.com, they attract over half a million visitors monthly. The websites offer a wide variety of features, helpful information and personal services.

Dedicated to The Light of Intuition
Sri V. Krishnaswamy—mentor and friend
With thanks to Julie, Joram, Isaac and Janelle

Welcome from
Dadhichi

Dear Friend,

Welcome! It's great to have you here, reading your horoscope, trying to learn more about yourself and what's in store for you in 2010.

I visited Mexico a while ago and stumbled upon the Mayan prophecies for 2012, which, they say, is the year when the longstanding calendar we use in the western world supposedly stops! If taken literally, some people could indeed believe that 'the end of the world is near'. However, I see it differently.

Yes, it might seem as though the world is getting harder and harder to deal with, especially when fear enters our lives. But, I believe that 'the end' indicated by these Mayan prophecies has more to do with the end that will create new beginnings for our societies, more to do with making changes to our material view of life and some necessary adjustments for the human race to progress and prosper in future. So let's get one thing straight: you and I will both be around after 2012, reading our 2013 horoscopes!

My prediction and advice centres around keeping a cool mind and not reacting to the fear that could overtake us. Of course, this isn't easy, especially when media messages might increase our anxiety about such things as the impacts of global warming or the scarcity of fossil fuels.

I want you to understand that it is certainly important to be aware and play your part in making the world a better place; however, the best and surest way to support global goals is to help yourself first. Let me explain. If everyone focused just a little more on improving *themselves* rather than just pointing their finger to criticise others, it would result in a dramatic change and improvement; not just globally, but societally. And, of course, you mustn't forget what a positive impact this would have on your personal relationships as well.

Astrology focuses on self-awareness; your own insights into your personality, thinking processes and relationships. This is why this small book you have in your hand doesn't only concentrate on what is going to happen, but more importantly how you can *make* things happen positively through being your best.

I have always said that there are two types of people: puppets and actors. The first simply react to each outside stimulus and are therefore slaves of their environment, and even of their own minds and emotions. They are puppets in the hands of karma. The other group I call actors. Although they can't control what happens to them all the time, either, they are better able to adapt and gain something purposeful in their lives. They are in no way victims of circumstance.

I hope you will use what is said in the following pages to become the master of your destiny, and not rely on the predictions that are given as mere fate but as valuable guidelines to use intelligently when life presents you with its certain challenges.

Neither the outside world, nor the ups and downs that occur in your life, should affect your innermost spirituality and self-confidence. Take control: look beyond your current challenges and use them as the building blocks of experience to create success and fulfilment in the coming year.

I believe you have the power to become great and shine your light for all to see. I hope your 2010 horoscope book will be a helpful guide and inspiration for you.

Warm regards, and may the stars shine brightly for you in 2010!

Your Astrologer,

Dadhichi Toth

Contents

The Libra
Identity

If you are not willing to risk the unusual, you will have to settle for the ordinary.

—Jim Rohn

Libra: A Snapshot

Key Characteristics

Refined, social, artistic, vacillating, intellectual, communicative, concerned with relationships

Compatible Star Signs

Gemini, Leo, Sagittarius, Aquarius

Key Life Phrase

I interact

Platinum Assets

Tremendous charm, persuasive ability and social popularity

Life Goals

To find harmony and balance in all relationships

Zodiac Totem

The Scales of Justice

Zodiac Symbol

Zodiac Facts

Seventh sign of the zodiac; movable, barren, masculine, dry

Element

Air

Famous Librans

Barbara Walters, Hugh Jackman, Kate Winslet, Julio Iglesias, Brigitte Bardot, Michael Douglas, Will Smith, Olivia Newton-John, Susan Sarandon, Gwyneth Paltrow, Richard Harris, Neve Campbell, Sting, David Lee Roth, Alicia Silverstone, Sigourney Weaver, Matt Damon, Luke Perry, John Lennon, Jean-Claude Van Damme, John Lithgow

Libra: Your profile

Being born under the seventh sign of the zodiac, you are the consummate 'people person'. Always curious and ready to make the effort to gain an insight into any sort of human relationship, the human mind and personality fascinates you.

There are times, however, when this almost compelling desire to be with others can overtake you, making you highly dependent on having company. But you have a fine intellect and great communication skills, so this desire shouldn't be a problem as long as you learn to balance your needs against the needs of others. And, of course, this is the primary life lesson for you, which is well depicted by your symbol, the scales.

People always flock to you in a social situation. They love to hear your stories; the way in which you share your understanding of the world and the events that have helped shape you.

You have the gift of the gab—there's no doubt about that—and even when you have to say something that's rather unpalatable, you can somehow sweeten the words that come out of your mouth. How can it happen that, even when someone is being insulting, they can still be so popular? That's the Libran way. You really do have a talent for speaking your mind while not offending others.

Balance and discrimination are two of the most important aspects of your character. You're able to see every side of the story and will therefore never do something you feel is unjust or will disadvantage someone else. However, at times, you're the one who is disadvantaged through this process.

You know, you mustn't live your life fearing you're going to offend anyone. At times, when you have to choose between warring parties, choices becomes awfully difficult and divided loyalties could be the result. This is the flipside of the coin of these Libran talents.

Indecision is a problem for many Librans and, because you like to get feedback from different sources before making up your mind, the contradictory stories that you hear may make your conclusions a long, drawn-out process. Self-reliance is an essential part of your journey and is something you should also strive to achieve. This is the only way you will empower yourself and bring out the highest self within you.

You're ruled by Venus, which is loving, caring and tasteful in every sense. People see you as a class act. Sharing and generosity is another part of your personality that wins over others. You're full of magnetic charm and friends are never a problem for you to find.

Living a life of harmony and peace is a must for every Libran. If you find yourself in an environment that is abrasive and contrary to your need for equilibrium, you will not feel well and will do anything you can to immediately remove yourself from that situation. Venus is again responsible for your need for tranquil living and working spaces. The gracious and feminine energies will always bring to the fore the softer side of your personality. This is seen in the way you dress, you cook, how you furnish your home and generally live your life.

Librans are fun to be around. Likewise, you always want to surround yourself with those who have a good sense of humour and who like to party and share ideas of an intellectual nature. Your search for personal happiness is bound up in relationships. Part of your search is centred on meeting as many interesting people as you can so you find that perfect match in life.

Finding your soulmate will lead you along the many highways and byways of life and, therefore, Librans are usually quite experienced in the ways of life, love and human interaction. This makes you somewhat philosophical as well, if you are one of the more evolved types born under this star sign.

Three classes of Libra

There are three kinds of Libran. It's important to understand which of these categories you fall under because, within any given star sign, there are nuances of character. So let's see what marks you out as different from your other Libran brothers and sisters.

If you happen to be born between the 24th of September and the 3rd of October, you bring out the traits of Libra fully. Due to the very powerful ruling of Venus over your life and character, artistic, compassionate and social activities will predominate in your life. You'll also have many, many friends and loving them unconditionally will be what you strive for. Just don't lose yourself in the mish-mash of social events that comes from being with too many people at once. It is imperative for you to learn to stand on your own two feet and not accept that what everyone is saying to you is 100 per cent correct. You may have a certain amount of gullibility that needs to be overcome.

For those of you in Libra born between the 4th and the 13th of October, there is an element of zaniness flowing through your veins. Some might call you a little bit crazy, but it's all in good fun, isn't it, Libra? You do have the tendency to change your mind erratically and this can leave people wondering what your plans are. Try to think through your goals firmly and decisively before acting upon any decisions. You may be prone to dropping your life circumstances and even relationships at a moment's notice for the attraction of bigger and better things.

Those of you born between the 14th and the 23rd of October are constantly seeking out truth and knowledge. This will make you a perennial student, always on the hunt for facts and figures. Learning and understanding yourself, the world and its people generally, is governed by Mercury's co-rulership of you and your personality. Because of this as well, you are forever young and some might even say you suffer a bit of the 'Peter Pan syndrome', meaning you never grow up.

Libra role model: Barbara Walters

The world-famous journalist and first-rate interviewer Barbara Walters was born under your star sign of Libra. When we say that Libra is keenly interested in human psychology and what makes others tick, Barbara would have to epitomise this Libran spirit. She has her own recognisable brand of style, which she has created by using her incredible ability to communicate and understand others, and bringing that knowledge to the world at large.

Libra: The light side

If ever there was a list of people to call up to come to a party for fun and generally a great night out, you, Libra, would have to be on the top of that list. Because Venus rules you, it infuses you with such magnetic appeal, charm and humour. In fact, you don't even have to open your mouth and people are attracted to your warm, bubbly energy. Once you do start to speak, however, others will become addicted to your personality.

You probably didn't make a conscious effort on stylishness and sophistication because they seem to have been born into you. Never mind the socio-economic climate in which you grew up; having Venus as your benefactor is definitely a lifelong boon because it does endow you with natural ability in social graces, etiquette and other great interactive skills. This will always be a benefit to you, not just in the realm of friendships but in your professional life as well.

You're a great judge of character, even though at times you are a little bit gullible. You will overcome this and eventually become a wonderful and insightful person who can see the many nuances of human character. You also have the uncanny ability to step outside your own personal bias and see a situation from every possible angle. This is truly a unique gift that very few people but Libra possess.

Libra: The shadow side

You should never, ever try to please too many people, Libra! The end result will be that you'll never please anyone at all, including yourself. The fact is that Libra tries to be all things to all people and thereby entangles themselves in intricate situations that are hard to get out of.

Speaking the plain and honest truth needs to be foremost in your mind when dealing with others, even if it means hurting someone's feelings or losing them, perhaps, as a friend. Diplomacy is one thing but hanging onto situations and relationships because of a fear or insecurity is never a good thing.

One of your most formidable traits is your desire to share the good things that happen to you. But, unfortunately, others are sometimes envious and your impulse to tell everyone all the details of what's happening in your life might come across as boastful and exaggerative. Try a little harder to put yourself in other people's shoes to understand how they are seeing you.

Libra woman

Women born under Libra are usually stylish, classy and elegant people who seem to have a natural affinity with femininity. Venus as your ruler is the main reason that your loving, graceful and attractive energies are in such abundance.

The female Libran personality can really bedazzle others, and not just in major social circumstances but even in the smaller, day-to-day circumstances of life. Your smile, open-hearted and natural communication style wins the hearts of everyone around you.

You have a magic touch with even the most mundane tasks and like to bring life to anything you do. Having an artistic leaning, you enjoy fabrics, relaxing environments, perfumes and anything that can make you feel and look good but which also offer you the opportunity to express that wonderful creativity of yours.

Libra is about harmony and females born under this star sign really do like to take a gentle and loving attitude into the world to make things better for others. Friends and relatives will always look to you to help them sort through their troubles because they know you have the capacity to break down a problem into its constituent parts and justly look at what needs to be done without any thought of your own personal gain.

Because Venus represents love and marriage, you are endowed with a natural inclination towards these things. Libran women are natural-born lovers and the partner who is fortunate enough to attract you into their lives will be treated like royalty by their Libran female consort.

The other reason that love is so important to you is because of the component of communication, upon which all Libran women place great emphasis. You have a deep-seated need to express how you feel and also expect the same in return from those with whom you live and work.

Usually in the early stages of your life, you might try a little too hard to be accepted. There's nothing worse than being rejected socially and this, if not understood and handled well by you, could result in long-term emotional scarring. So be it. But you should never compromise yourself for the sake of saying that you have a few extra friends. This will damage your spirit, without doubt.

Due to their habit of being with so many people, some Libran women fear being alone. My suggestion is for you to learn to savour your own company; meditate a little on the higher principles of your inner self and then you'll realise that, when all is said and done, you are your own best friend (or your own worst enemy). This will afford you the peace of mind that you truly aspire to as a Libran.

Don't get your hands dirty with other people's problems when you're not invited to. Your sense of justice may tempt you to assist others when in fact all you will be doing is stirring up even more trouble. Of course, if someone requests your help, do so in your typical Libran way; but once the job is done, disappear just as quickly.

Libra is the sign of balance and, because you are represented by the scales of justice, you have an instinctive belief in the laws of karma. Very few are actually able to implement this life principle in practice but you, Libra, being a woman of the world and the spirit, understand exactly what this means.

Libra man

The Libran man is an unusual mix of masculinity and femininity. On the one hand, the sign of Libra is classified as a masculine zodiac sign. Yet on the other hand, Venus, the most feminine of the planets, is the ruler of Libra. Due to this fact, most Libran males are what you would call 'connected' to the feminine side of their personalities.

Due to this deep inner balance of male and female traits, you have an excellent advantage in the world, especially if you're dealing with women at large. Females feel comfortable in your presence and realise that, even if subliminally you have some interest in them, you're always most gracious and tasteful in the way you go about it. Generally, however, you really do enjoy the company of women and are not afraid to admit that you probably have more female than male friends.

As a Libran-born man, you are suave, sophisticated and, some might even say, 'a ladies' man'. This can at times present you with difficulties, especially in your choice of partners. You may enjoy playing the field only to find yourself overrun with opportunities and then not quite knowing which one to choose. You should always be honest with others and not lead them on.

You have a wonderful sense of humour and know how to use this in every department of your life. You are the master of words and know how to string sentences together to extract the maximum benefit and response from your peers and strangers alike. Because of your ability to persuade others along certain lines of thought, you make an excellent diplomat, salesperson or teacher.

You're a very well-read person and pride yourself on having a broad base of knowledge and interests. You like current affairs, history, music and even philosophical studies. If you do take to some sporting activities, you most definitely need to do something which allows you to use some of your brainpower as well as your muscular strength.

Because relationships fascinate you, you try to learn as much about them as you can. To you, attracting others is a science, not a hit-and-miss affair. You are very idealistic about friendships and, if someone doesn't meet that standard, you are extremely disappointed. A word of advice, though: first you need to be beyond reproach in your own ethics and integrity if you expect others to be.

Some Libran men are never content with what they have, believing that a never-ending search for perfection will somehow land them their imaginary ideal. However, it is wise to try to be happy with what you have, even if you still continue to look a little more.

Become firmer in your decision making. Don't rely on others to tell you which way to travel. Trust your heart, your instinct and your higher wisdom, with which you are well blessed. Once you learn to trust the inner faculty of your own intuition, you'll be able to make much more efficient and successful decisions in your personal and business lives.

Libra child

Libran children are the darlings of the zodiac. Who can help but fall in love with a child of Venus, the ruling planet of Libra? Your Libran child is naturally affectionate, communicative and inquisitive.

To bring out the best in your Libran child, first and foremost you need to get some basics of your own lifestyle in order. You see, a Libran child needs the most harmonious and loving environment in which to thrive. If you're reading this and you're having difficulties in your marriage, your work or other relationships that may impact upon the development of your Libran baby, you need to remedy it immediately! This will have a very, very powerful impact on the emotional and mental development of your child.

The Libran child needs to feel as though they have a soft place to land. They need to feel loved, nurtured and understood. In some ways, the Libran child requires more time and attention than any other typical child their age. Sure, all children need to believe their parents can go the extra mile, but the Libran child, being born under the element of air, is exceedingly curious and is not satisfied with superficial answers to any of the questions they may ask of you. Be prepared to go into detail and understand that, at the same time, this has an extraordinarily beneficial effect on them. You should be proud that they ask these questions and are so mature for their age.

Because Libran children have a natural flair for art, music, dance and other aesthetic activities, it's not a bad idea to have part of their room set up to be used exclusively this way. Get them involved in creative processes and, once you commit yourself to doing this, you will see they can take to such hobbies and activities like a fish to water. Many young Libran children are artistically gifted.

Children born under the air signs are particularly highly strung because of their predisposition towards over-thinking. Teach them to take regular exercise, to regulate their breathing, and to get adequate rest and a good diet. The balance of all these factors will ensure your child grows up to be a well-integrated human being.

Romance, love and marriage

Love, romance, sensuality and even sexuality are synonymous with the word 'Libra'! It just can't be any other way because Venus so strongly regulates everything you do in life that it's part and parcel of your make-up to desire love and be an expert at showing it as well.

I often say that one of the key phrases for Libra is 'it's better to be unhappily in love than not in love at all'. Unfortunately, this is precisely the reason why many Librans—although they are endowed with such loving and affectionate ways—fail to fulfil this aspect of their lives.

A few slight changes in your attitude will bring you much more happiness in this area of your life. You love to show affection but are often too quick and trusting and realise all too late that you've given your heart to the wrong person. You're an idealist by birth and therefore, anyone and everyone you meet seems to be so much more than what they really are. Step back, use those wonderful Libran powers of discrimination that you possess, and then make your decision. This is the first law of love for any Libran who wishes to be successful.

Librans want their cake and they want to eat it, too. By this I mean that once you find someone with whom you can share your heart, try not to be too concerned about holding onto each and every one of your other social relationships. You have the tendency to want to live a life of diversity, variety, popularity and, unfortunately, not everyone can do this as well as you, Libra. A committed one on one relationship may not be all that easy for you, at least not in the early part of your life. Try to sow your wild oats early and quickly so you can then get down to the business of satisfying yourself in the deeper aspects of love.

Once you become involved in love you can be a very loyal person, but you need assurance that your loyalty is a two-way street. You also want to know your love will be reciprocated, and so I recommend to any Libran they should avoid involving themselves with anyone who is not tactile and expressive of their love, too. A plant needs water to survive and, in the same way, Libra needs a practical demonstration of love to feel fulfilled in life.

In matters of sexuality and intimacy, you are exploratory and also need someone with whom you can share the adventure of love. You need the physical excitement as well as intellectual and emotional depth. You want it all, Libra! There's nothing worse for a Libran than feeling bored in the bedroom. Once this happens, it's very hard to regain their heart.

Thus it's very important for you to select your life partner with due diligence, even at times clinical analysis, to make sure you don't spend your life with someone who is not going to fulfil all of these criteria so essential for a Libran to feel fully satisfied on every level of their being.

Once married, a Libran will pour everything they have into the family, making sure that the home is full of warmth, a loving atmosphere, and all the material security needed to bring happiness to their loved ones.

Health, wellbeing and diet

Overindulgence is the first word that comes to mind when I look to advise a Libran on what to avoid if they wish to have a healthy life. Venus has the tendency to spur you on to doing things excessively. This includes your eating and general lifestyle habits. Try to be more mindful of doing things in moderation and this problem won't arise.

You're quite capable of tuning into your body's signals. Your health is really simply a matter of taking responsibility for your own wellbeing rather than relying on others to tell you what to do, what tablets to take for what ailment, etcetera. In this way you can bypass problems well before they arise. It is possible for most Librans to make their own life-style adjustments.

Yours is an air sign and therefore your thinking may also have much to do with how well or unwell you feel physically. Take a step back and listen to what's going on in your mind right now. Do you hear all the chattering going on—the mental feedback you're giving yourself? If the chatter must happen, make sure you're directing it into positive lines of thinking. Librans should never hold a grudge or let their emotions get the better of them and this is one way, through simple mental observation, that you can bring your physical, emotional and mental energies into a harmonious alignment.

The kidneys and bladder are ruled by the sign of Libra. These parts of your body are likely to be constitutionally weak and will be the first point of breakdown if you don't look after yourself with good exercise, an excellent diet and a balanced lifestyle.

Eating organic fresh fruits and vegetables have a tonic effect on your system and can help release toxins that are the cause of disease. Plenty of fresh water, freshly squeezed juices and, don't forget, being an air sign, deep, rhythmic breathing is essential as an adjunct to good health.

Some of the fruits and vegetables that are excellent for Libran-born individuals are melon, yellow fruits such as banana, organic rice, raw milk and yoghurt. This will supply you ample vitamins and minerals to help you on the path of physical well-being. In all cases, try to avoid processed foods of any sort or at least minimise their intake.

Work

As long as you can work in a field that involves you with others, with people with whom you can communicate and serve, you'll be 'as happy as a pig in mud'. If that's not the case, you could find yourself becoming frustrated, and that energy could then turn into anger and other negative emotions. Therefore, Libra, at the outset of your working life, try to move along social pathways that allow you to shine your best talents of diplomacy and verbal or other communication skills in advisory or healing roles.

Human relations, sales and marketing are excellent professional domains in which you'll find great satisfaction and also substantial material returns for your efforts.

The second thing is that, once you do find yourself in a field of work you enjoy, your co-workers and the company you keep will either augment or diminish your satisfaction. Only work with people with whom you feel comfortable and who have a shared interest in your success as well.

Your ruling planet Venus endows you with tremendous artistic and creative skills. Even if you happen to work in banking or another commercial sector of society, you will still be able to bring to bear upon your duties a touch of elegance and artistic flair that will set you apart from others, thereby ensuring a successful professional path for you.

Key to karma, spirituality and emotional balance

The key Libran phrase is 'I interact'. You have the ability to deal with a diverse range of people and situations. Exchanging ideas is crucial to your personal development.

Karmically speaking, your big challenge is to find balance between your needs and the needs of others. Giving yourself time is as important, if not more important, than the time you give to others.

Make decisions in the quietude of reflection on your own inner self. By all means, listen to the input of others, but sift through what you hear and then come to a firm conclusion and stick to your guns.

You can open your heart and develop yourself spiritually by using such oils as jasmine, myrrh and orange. Wednesdays, Fridays and Saturdays are excellent days to meditate and connect with your higher self.

Your lucky days

Your luckiest days are Wednesday, Friday and Saturday.

Your lucky numbers

Remember that the forecasts given later in the book will help you optimise your chances of winning. Your lucky numbers are:

6, 15, 24, 33, 42, 51

8, 17, 26, 35, 44, 53

5, 14, 23, 32, 41, 50

Your destiny years

Your most important years are 6, 15, 24, 33, 42, 51, 60, 78 and 87.

Star Sign
Compatibility

Find a guy who calls you 'beautiful' instead of 'hot',
who calls you back when you hang up on him, who will
lie under the stars and listen to your heartbeat, or will
stay awake just to watch you sleep... Wait for the boy
who kisses your forehead, who wants to show you off to
the world when you are in sweats, who holds your hand
in front of his friends, who thinks you're just as pretty
without makeup on. One who is constantly reminding
you of how much he cares and how lucky he is to have
you... The one who turns to his friends and says,
'That's her'.

—Anonymous

Romantic compatibility

How compatible are you with your current partner, lover or friend? Did you know that astrology can reveal a whole new level of understanding between people simply by looking at their star sign and that of their partner? In this chapter I'd like to share some special insights that will help you better appreciate your strengths and challenges using Sun sign compatibility.

The Sun reflects your drive, willpower and personality. The essential qualities of two star signs blend like two pure colours, producing an entirely new colour. Relationships, similarly, produce their own emotional colours when two people interact. The following is a general guide to your romantic prospects with others and how, by knowing the astrological 'colour' of each other, the art of love can help you create a masterpiece.

Quick-reference guide: Horoscope compatibility between signs (percentage)

	Aries	Taurus	Gemini	Cancer	Leo	Virgo	Libra	Scorpio	Sagittarius	Capricorn	Aquarius	Pisces
Aries	60	65	70	65	90	45	70	80	90	50	55	65
Taurus	60	70	70	80	70	90	75	85	50	95	80	85
Gemini	70	70	75	60	80	75	90	60	75	50	90	50
Cancer	65	80	60	75	70	75	60	95	55	45	70	50
Leo	90	70	80	70	85	75	65	75	45	45	70	90
Virgo	45	90	75	75	75	70	80	75	70	95	50	70
Libra	70	75	90	60	65	80	80	65	95	85	95	75
Scorpio	80	85	60	95	75	85	85	75	80	65	60	90
Sagittarius	90	50	75	55	95	70	80	95	85	55	60	50
Capricorn	50	95	50	45	45	95	85	45	55	85	70	85
Aquarius	55	80	90	70	70	50	95	75	70	70	80	55
Pisces	65	85	50	90	75	70	50	75	90	50	55	80

When reading the following I ask you to remember that no two star signs are ever totally incompatible. With effort and compromise, even the most 'difficult' astrological matches can work. Don't close your mind to the full range of life's possibilities! Learning about each other and ourselves is the most important facet of astrology.

Each star sign combination is followed by the elements of those star signs and the result of their combining. For instance, Aries is a fire sign and Aquarius is an air sign and this combination produces a lot of 'hot air'. Air feeds fire and fire warms air. In fact, fire requires air. However, not all air and fire combinations work. I have included information about the different birth periods within each star sign and this will throw even more light on your prospects for a fulfilling love life with any star sign you choose.

Good luck in your search for love, and may the stars shine upon you in 2010!

Compatibility quick-reference guide

Each of the twelve star signs has a greater or lesser affinity with one another. The quick-reference guide will show you who's hot and who's not so hot as far as your relationships are concerned.

LIBRA + ARIES
Air + Fire = Hot Air

The combination of Libra and Aries is an interesting

one, with both of you being opposites in the zodiac. Although astrologers generally believe opposites attract, this is both true and not so true in the case of yourself and Aries.

Yes, the power and energy of Aries is certainly attractive to you and their up-front and daring nature brings a few sparks into your life. However, you like peace and will never, under any circumstance, tolerate the abrasiveness of Aries for too long. Aries is aggressive and this, in some strange way, inspires your sensual nature.

Love for Libra and Aries is somewhat unconventional because although you want peace and harmony, Aries is always on the go and restless by nature. Aries' straightforward and honest nature is sometimes a little hard for you to resist. You like the energy and the aura they exude and can sometimes feel a little overpowered by them. Aries is able to utilise your social skills to bring themselves down a few notches to enjoy life at a more leisurely pace by being in your company.

One thing you do like about Aries is the fact that they're enthusiastic and prepared to explore sex and intimacy with you. Because you're such a sensual person yourself, you feel energised and nurtured by Aries. At times, however, Aries does tend to be a little insensitive to your emotional needs and this is something you'll need to teach them over time.

Both of you are creative individuals but Aries likes to take the lead and you'll have to get used to the fact that their egos are quite sensitive to them being usurped by others. As long as you let them think they are in control, then all should go well in the Libra–Aries relationship.

The success of your relationship with Aries will depend on the pace and level of comfort you develop with each other over time. As long as they co-operate and discuss their feelings with you in a rational way there's still a great opportunity to develop a wonderful romance with them.

You have a lovely synchronicity with Aries born between the 21st and the 30th of March. Both of you are attracted to each other and these individuals are extremely strong-willed but also protective at the same time. Because you're so interested in family and a safe haven in which to make your life, these Arians will fulfil that need within you.

You're better off as a friend with an Aries born between the 31st of March and the 10th of April. You might attempt romance but will find a few areas that don't particularly gel between you. Take your time to savour the friendship rather than pushing into areas where neither of you feel comfortable.

With Aries born between the 11th and the 20th of April, you have a better intellectual rapport than a physical one. Your discussions and social life will be fulfilling to both of you and through this keen understanding of each other's needs, you'll be able to resolve some of your differences.

LIBRA + TAURUS
Air + Earth = Dust

If you've been looking for someone to bring your indecisiveness into a more steady state, you'll find that Taurus is probably one of the best zodiac signs to do this.

Because you are both ruled by Venus, you have an instinctive feel for each other's needs. However, Taurus is much more grounded than you are, and will serve you well both on the practical, day-to-day level and with your emotions as well.

Again, being ruled by Venus, you are particularly sensual and sensitive to your environment and the company you keep. You'll be pleased to note that Taurus also thinks exactly like this, too. Therefore, your day-to-day affairs and your social engagements will inspire you both and give you a common objective together.

Taurus may not be so comfortable with the fact that at times you are rather casual and, indeed, fickle. In anything but matters of love, Taurus will cope with that, but Taurus needs to know you are 100 per cent committed and will not deviate from your relationship once you've given them your heart. By doing so, you'll have a rich and mutually satisfying relationship with them.

The two of you can achieve much in life, with the air sign of Libra being the brains of the team and Taurus being the practical, earthy, doer of the match. This combination of air and earth often achieves good financial security, along with emotional satisfaction.

Some astrologers believe that this is not a particularly great match, especially with Taurus being as inflexible as they are in some of their opinions. On the other hand, you well know, Libra, how you like balance and can easily see another person's point of view. If Taurus gets stuck in these inflexible attitudes, this might not be all that good for your relationship because you will be exasperated.

Also, at times, there is a conflict between your personal and social obligations, which could leave you wondering whether or not you are quite ready to settle down together. Therefore, reasonable compromises need to be made along the way, and I suggest that you never, under any circumstances, marry out of a sense of obligation.

However, there are exceptions to the rule, and with Taureans born between the 21st and the 29th of April, it's likely you'll fall head over heels in love with them. This match has the hallmarks of great physical passion, love and affection within it.

With Taureans born between the 30th of April and the 10th of May, there's also a good synchronicity between you. However, they are a little more concerned about finances and, unless you have a lot of money, you might find this is an obstacle to taking the relationship to the next level. Sort out your money issues before committing yourselves.

If you team up with a Taurean born between the 11th and the 21st of May, you may find their slow and steady thinking a little too challenging for you. They're also quite inflexible in their routine, which will frustrate you as well.

LIBRA + GEMINI
Air + Air = Wind

Libra and Gemini are well suited intellectually, and in most other areas of life, too, the two of you will sit comfortably and do well as a partnership. For this reason, it's a great omen for the long term.

Venus and Mercury rule Libra and Gemini respectively and are astrologically friendly. These are called 'benefic' planets and, therefore, a considerable amount of luck is destined to come your way if you pair up with a Gemini lover. You each resonate easily with the other's personality, and your need for learning, communication and general curiosity for life will be fulfilled in each other.

There's also a strong karmic connection between the two of you and so you understand each other, even without words, although talk will be the cornerstone of your love life.

With Libra being somewhat indecisive and airy-fairy and Gemini being continually on the go and perhaps a little too frenetic at times, there is a danger that this relationship might be spread too thinly in too many different directions. Do you actually have enough time for each other, is the question? Nevertheless, there'll be much excitement in your relationship together and you will constantly look forward to each other's company.

You're quite spiritual in the way you view life and love and may need to temper the 'butterfly effect' of Gemini. They do have a tendency to be here, there and everywhere and, in your opinion, are a little superficial. Sexually, you are quite compatible with Gemini, enjoying high-spirited conversation because you also believe that communication is the main ingredient of a successful relationship.

Geminis born between the 22nd of May and the 1st of June are extremely attracted to you and vice versa. You should, however, be aware that these Geminis have a tendency to be very highly strung and, although great multi-taskers, they don't often have enough time in their diaries for deep and committed relationships such as yours. This means you may not really be able to spend the quality time you'd like with them.

If you happen to meet someone born between the 2nd and the 12th of June, you can expect a wonderful romantic relationship with them. Venus, which is your ruling planet, has a large part to play in their lives and you'll automatically notice their deep affection and love as part of their character. They're interested in marriage and long-term commitment and they're also very affectionate and artistic people. Their great wit and interesting communication style is contagious and addictive for Libra.

Geminis born between the 13th and 21st of June are exciting and love to socialise. This is in keeping with your own character and, therefore, we could say that the two of you are almost ideally suited. Doing unusual things together and exploring the exotic and even bizarre side of life will give you great pleasure and wisdom. An important link between you is cultural exchange and travel.

LIBRA + CANCER
Air + Water = Rain

The two of you are on very different life paths. This should be said up-front before getting your hopes up too high for a Libra–Cancer match. Such a combination, astrologically and romantically speaking, is not considered ideal. But don't lose heart: there's always a chance to make things work if you practise some understanding.

You operate primarily from an intellectual level, while Cancer is wholly and solely a creature of emotion. Together this just doesn't gel and you'll be fed up with trying to deal with Cancer's swinging moods, day in and day out. There's a considerable level of complexity that needs to be addressed when dealing with Cancer. At times Cancer is not amenable to explaining exactly how they feel, which will frustrate you.

There's a lesson in this for you, Libra, which is: try to listen with your heart rather than your head. You do have the capacity to extend yourself intuitively to feel what Cancer is saying and feeling, but that may be a difficult task because your mind is constantly chattering and you believe that discussion is the only way to resolve differences. There may need to be other approaches with Cancer.

Both of you have an intense love of home and family, and this is a particularly compatible aspect of your relationship. Try to work along these lines and you'll find much in common. You, Libra, have a wonderfully aesthetic sense, and this is good because colour, balance, mood and a comfortable environment in which to live and work sits well with Cancer, too, who loves to nurture and tend to the family. On this level, yes, you are both extremely compatible and loving towards each other.

Sexually there are good prospects between you as long as you each accept the other's means of expression. Accept Cancer's sensitive, emotional expressions as they appear, and hopefully in return they'll be prepared to listen to your chit-chat in the bedroom. Basically, you both want to be loved and express your love so that each feels nurtured and appreciated by the other in the relationship.

By teaming up with a Cancerian born between the 22nd of June and the 3rd of July, you'll realise just how sensitive they are. Be prepared to support them and emotionally tend to them without words. Demonstrate your feelings through gestures that are tactile, not just verbal. That will work wonders for the relationship.

A good combination is with Cancers born between the 4th and the 13th of July. Because they are ruled by Scorpio, they are very passionate and will satisfy your sexual needs. Mind you, they are also possessive and jealous as well as vindictive in the extreme, so you need to be very strongly committed to them.

You have very powerful karmic connections with Cancers born between the 14th and the 23rd of July. You learn many new life lessons, even spiritual ones which will create inner personality transformations for you, through your association with them. Generally, this relationship is predominantly a spiritual one, but you can still enjoy the other emotional and physical aspects of a relationship with them as well.

LIBRA + LEO
Air + Fire = Hot Air

As well as both being creative, you are star signs that can be great friends, too. Love that is based on this kind of friendship and camaraderie usually makes for a great combination. This is also an air and fire sign mix, which more often than not augurs a successful relationship on all three levels: mental, emotional and physical.

Because Leo is such a charismatic sign, you'll be very attracted to them. Being hugely warm-hearted, intelligent, generous and also the life of the party, you look up to them and feel as if you could spend your life with them.

Because Libra is at times sensitive to what others think and say, one drawback will be Leo's brutal honesty. If you ask for their opinion, be prepared to accept what comes your way with no soft punches.

Try as hard as you might to teach Leo diplomacy and sugarcoat what they have to say, you might be severely disappointed. Leo is not a particularly compromising sign, while Libra is.

Your attraction to each other is undeniable and often people will remark that there's a really great meeting of minds between you and your Leo partner. Your combined energies fascinate others and as a couple you'll be the life of the party. You're both excellent hosts and hostesses and this makes you sought after for any event or social engagement.

Sexually the combination is a good one as well, with your element of air fuelling the sensual and passionate fires of Leo. Leo does love to make their partner feel great and, because you are the type of individual who needs romantic sentimentality and appreciates tokens and gestures of a person's love, Leo will satisfy you in this respect.

There's a good prospect for marriage or at least great friendship with Leos born between the 24th of July and the 4th of August. Your attraction is a two-way street, and you enjoy their rather unique way of thinking as well as the fact that they are quite independent individuals.

There could be some problems associated with Leos born between the 5th and the 14th of August. These Leos love change, travel and anything that has the mark of adventure. If you are the sort of individual who likes to drop everything at a moment's notice, then a relationship with someone in this category of Leo will suit you down to the ground.

More often than not, your sexual relationship with Leo is excellent; however, those born between the 15th and the 23rd of August may not be quite as compatible in this respect. Because Aries and the ruling planet Mars dominates them, their passion may be a little too overwhelming for you. You will have great friendship with them and, at least for some period of time, a wonderful sexual connection.

LIBRA + VIRGO
Air + Earth = Dust

Just because Virgo is shy and reluctant to express openly what they feel doesn't at all mean they are shallow and uncommitted once they do give their heart to someone. In this instance, it is you who may be a little too frivolous for their taste.

Your outgoing personality, which is constantly connecting with different people, could be alarming for Virgo, who might think you don't have the same level of commitment as they do. But fortunately your ruling planets Venus and Mercury are friendly in the astrological scheme of things, so there's a very easygoing and natural connection that hopefully will help you both overcome your concerns in this relationship.

The one thing Virgo will have to understand and to foster is the need to bite their tongue, even when they feel it's absolutely essential to criticise you. They probably don't realise just how sensitive you are and how important it is for you to be accepted and loved. Their caustic analysis of your personality might be too much for you to handle.

You have a great level of communication with Virgo, mainly because they are curious, intellectual types and like to analyse anything and everything deeply. That's okay, but if they choose to analyse you, you have no problem as long as they keep it light and breezy. It won't always be easy for them, though!

Virgo, unknown to many, is a dominant sign and likes to control others in a most subtle manner. Your fickle and socially varied lifestyle may not sit well with them and therefore you could have a problem if they try to constrain you.

With Virgo's practical and efficient manner and your social and aesthetic skills, the combination can be an excellent one if the relationship goes to the next stage. But, first things, first. You love spontaneous action, whereas Virgo always has a plan, which, at times, is a little inflexible. Adjustments and concessions for each other will need to be made before you commit.

Both of you enjoy sensuality but Virgo takes a little while to warm to your natural expressiveness in the bedroom. Once Virgo feels secure with you, however, you will realise that they too have a very strong sexual nature that needs to be fulfilled. As long as you give them structure, this friendship will move to the next stage.

Involving yourself in a relationship with Virgos born between the 24th of August and the 2nd of September will result in a good match and these individuals are not quite as critical as you would expect of Virgo. Your communication will flow quite easily with them.

Virgos born between the 3rd and 12th of September are a deeper and more serious type of individual and may not be as social as you would like them to be. In fact, these Virgos are sometimes loners who prefer more of a solitary lifestyle. This is not at all in keeping with a Libran's outgoing style.

Virgos born between the 13th and the 23rd of September are an excellent match for you. They are tactile and also enjoy sexual interactions. Their progressive, sexual ways will keep you on your toes, that's for sure!

LIBRA + LIBRA
Air + Air = Wind

In this relationship, you might find your ideal star twin because you both understand exactly what you want from each other. There's a soft and loving type of energy that results from two Librans involving themselves together.

Love, art, culture and other social aptitudes are marked in both of you and this brings to the fore great teamwork and social fun. As long as you keep a balance between the enjoyable aspects of life and the more serious responsibilities of work, finance and family requirements, this can be an excellent combination for you.

At times you are both restless and, indeed, although Libra is the sign of balance, as individuals you still need someone who can act as a counterbalance to your restless nature. Therefore, one of you is going to have to take the lead. You find it difficult to stay still or be decisive. There's a danger that boredom might set in and you won't actually achieve anything for the long term with each other. Try to make decisions and stick to them.

Another important feature of your relationship is based upon your incessant need for harmony and a peaceful life. Because you both value peace and non-confrontation so much, it's likely that if you aren't satisfied with any aspect of each other you might not want to raise the issue, even though you're both great communicators and love to delve into relationships and how they can be improved. You see, Libra is often insecure about relationships, and if you feel as though someone is a formidable match, you don't want to do anything that might risk the status quo with them.

Expect a really busy timetable with another Libran. Your life is already full, so trying to adjust to each other's diaries might be part of the problem in solidifying your love for each other. Make time to discuss ways of being together to grow the relationship.

Generally, the sexual relationship between two Librans is excellent and covers all bases, including the physical, mental and emotional components.

True love results from a relationship with another Libran born between the 24th of September and the 4th of October. All your dreams can be fulfilled by them. Because you're dominated by Venus, love and affection are the bases of your friendship. Your sexual lives will also be fulfilling.

A relationship that is unexpected and quite different is quite likely with a Libran born between the 5th and the 13th of October. If a day-to-day, traditional existence is what you want, then these individuals may not be the type of person you want to get involved with. Some of them are footloose and fancy-free.

You have a wonderful intellectual rapport if you team up with a Libran born between the 14th and the 23rd of October. Both of you are very much in tune and enjoy each other's company. You can work as well as be creative together and, further-more, good humour and a bit of joke telling are key components of this match.

LIBRA + SCORPIO
Air + Water = Rain

Flattery, attention and all things romantic are

extremely important to the Libran temperament. Because of this, an association with Scorpio will satisfy you deeply because they know exactly how to turn on the romantic lights for the Libran personality.

This is an intense match and you mustn't have any delusions about just how moody, dominating and fiercely passionate the Scorpio character is. This will not be a lightweight relationship, by any stretch of the imagination. Superficially, you won't survive. You have to delve deeply with Scorpio to gain the most out of a romance with them.

Scorpio is the most sexually magnetic of the star signs, so they understand love and what's necessary to fuel its passionate fires. But on the other hand, Scorpio can be possessive, domineering and demanding, and these aspects are something that Libra finds difficult to deal with. They demand your absolute loyalty and because you are a free, socially independent individual, this will bog down the relationship.

Scorpio fascinates you because they are philosophical, intense and deep. They are excellent communicators, but not all the time. They love to use silence, both as a means of enticing others and punishing them as well. This deep and still energy of Scorpio is a double-edged sword.

No doubt Libra and Scorpio are powerfully linked sexually and the Venus–Mars combination of your signs reflects the archetypal male–female relationship. As a result you'll enjoy your physical contact and can fulfil each other's wildest dreams.

You can expect an excellent relationship with Scorpios born between the 24th of October and the 2nd of November. Because they are born on the border of Libra, they reflect some of your own Libran traits and therefore this is a great mental and sexual relationship. You see much of yourself in them and vice versa.

Scorpios born between the 3rd and the 12th of November are karmically difficult for you and a relationship with them will result in some pretty powerful lessons; some good and some bad. You'll need to jump in boots and all if you're going to be involved with these people. Because Neptune powerfully rules them, they may be rather difficult to understand; but this may also be part of the lure with these individuals.

Expect immense highs and lows with Scorpios born between the 13th and 22nd of November. The unpredictable Moon causes their moods to swing like a pendulum. Because you yourself are also somewhat changeable in nature, this relationship is in danger of creating far too many extremes emotionally.

LIBRA + SAGITTARIUS
Air + Fire = Hot Air

'Stimulating' is the best way to describe a relationship between you and a Sagittarian. This relationship is a great combination and one that will offer you fun, adventure and a whole lot of exciting experiences.

Your ruling planets of Venus and Jupiter are the finest of the zodiac and usually result in considerable good fortune when their forces are combined. Likewise, you and your Sagittarian partner will enjoy the benefits of these positive planetary vibrations on your relationship, even though the combination is probably not the best.

Like Sagittarius, you enjoy life but they are probably a little more hell-bent on maintaining their independence, which could be difficult for you if you're trying to tie them down to a long-term and committed relationship. Sagittarians are the masters of variety and excitement and feel uncomfortable if they're not on the move. You, Libra, also enjoy a high degree of independence and socialising, but Sagittarius would have to be far more reluctant to put down their roots than you are.

In your relationship with a Sagittarian, get ready to travel to some wonderful new places around the globe, meet unusual and intellectual people and generally explore avenues of life that you never thought existed. Sagittarius takes pride in the fact that they love to explore and discover new things and will want to share that with you.

A relationship with a Sagittarian is full of love and also generosity. Actually, the two of you could be quite wasteful and you could push yourselves to the limit. You might feel these effects particularly in the realm of sex or physical intimacy, with fiery Sagittarius stimulating every aspect of your being.

Sagittarians are rather blunt in the way they express themselves and, because you're so sensitive, you can only hope your Sagittarian partner develops some sort of etiquette that's not too abrasive for your Libran thin skin.

Those Sagittarians who have their birth date between the 23rd of November and the 1st of December are larger-than-life characters who have very big egos. To win their hearts, you simply need to feed that ego a little and you'll have them eating out of your hand.

If you choose a Sagittarian born between the 2nd and the 11th of December, get ready for some hot and heavy arguments with them. Being dominated by Mars and Aries shows that they have plenty of physical energy but they are also restless, impulsive types who need to develop more patience. This may not be the best of combinations, although you will feel very attracted to them.

You can expect a great relationship with any Sagittarian born between the 12th and the 22nd of December. These are the compassionate Sagittarians who will look after your each and every need, wanting to make sure you are content in every aspect. If you're looking for a loyal Sagittarian, those born between these dates are ideal for you as a choice in love.

LIBRA + CAPRICORN
Air + Earth = Dust

Not too many people are aware just how sexually orientated Capricorn is because initially they appear to be so conservative and withhold expressing themselves. But spend a little time with them and you'll soon see the softer and more expressive parts of their nature.

However long you need to wait might not be soon enough for you, Libra, because you need so much attention and TLC that waiting around for a Capricorn to show you this hidden side of their nature will quickly wear thin. On the other hand, if you're a patient sort of Libra, the wait could be well worth it.

Capricorn is realistic, practical and efficient with their use of time, money and, unfortunately, in your opinion, their emotions and affection. Capricorn might not feed your sentimental, loving nature to the extent that you would wish. And also, because your mind is creative and sometimes intangible in its tastes, Capricorn's materialistic view of life might not gel with your philosophy.

Capricorn works hard and will provide you with all the luxuries you want in life. If financial security is something you're looking for in a partner, Capricorn will absolutely satisfy this need, but at what cost?

You approach life with a spontaneous and devil-may-care attitude at times, whereas Capricorn is reluctant to show their hand. Some Capricorns are even solitary and don't like mixing, which would be a real shame because of your love of people, parties and humanity in general. If you choose to enter into a relationship with Capricorn, their desire to spend time alone may end up creating an almighty challenge for you.

Developing strong levels of intimacy and sexual honesty is also a stumbling block for Capricorn. You too may be traditional in your approach to lovemaking, but Capricorn is 'hardcore'—and not in the way you think!—I mean very, very traditional. Once you break through the surface ice, however, and prove to Capricorn that you're in it for the long haul, you'll be surprised—even startled—at just how nourishing and exciting they can be in the bedroom.

Choosing a relationship with a Capricorn born between the 23rd of December and the 1st of January will be extremely difficult for you to deal with. I suggest you hang in there, though, because once you show them some affection and love and allow them to trust you a little more, this relationship can be one that is very satisfying.

Your most compatible relationship with a Capricorn will be with those born between the 2nd and the 12th of January because these individuals have very strong communication skills, like yourself. They enjoy money, power and all of the luxuries and influence that these things bring, but it's important for them not to extend that into the relationship. If they try to control you, it could mean a quick exit on your part.

Don't let your sexual or emotional feelings be dictated by money or the material security that a Capricorn can offer you, especially if they happen to be born between the 13th and the 20th of January. Capricorns tend to make money easily and it would be a mistake for you to lean on them for your future financial security. Try to think beyond material gain.

LIBRA + AQUARIUS

Air + Air = Wind

A relationship between Libra and Aquarius is probably one of the best out of all the zodiac signs due to the fact that the element of air is common to both of you. Although for the most part Aquarius is misunderstood by other signs, you have a natural tendency to feel comfortable and connected with them, understanding them quite easily. A relationship with Aquarius is built on mutual admiration and deep intellectual insight.

A relationship with Aquarius propels you forward in a progressive way and, even though it may be a little too fast-paced for you—and unpredictable at that—you nevertheless enjoy this and find it very exciting.

Because Aquarius is so spontaneous, you'll be living on your nerves with them. Life will be a bag of unexpected events and this will fuel your desire for more of the same.

You're a very sensual creature by nature and

the experimental, somewhat avant-garde lovemaking of Aquarius is perfect for you. Not only are you great in bed together but the added bonus of being extremely close in friendship will make it hard for you to tear yourself away from this relationship.

The air signs have a tendency to want to communicate their ideas and therefore Libra and Aquarius will do so very easily. You'll keep the relationship alive by virtue of the fact that you'll leave no stone unturned intellectually.

Because of your unconventional views on love and marriage, you're both prepared to try something out of the ordinary. Even if you don't spend the rest of your life with your Aquarian partner, it's a relationship you'll never, ever forget and you'll always take something away from it in the way of wisdom.

Aquarians born between the 21st and the 30th of January are unusual characters and therefore you can expect a relationship that's completely beyond this world. You will be infatuated with each other; but you mustn't surround yourselves with a bubble by excluding your relatives and friends. Make this an inclusive relationship, one in which you can share the joys of your love with the other people in your lives.

Aquarians born between the 31st of January and the 8th of February are very well connected with you and this is a great karmic–spiritual combination. The psychological synchronicity between you is excellent and therefore your romance will develop quite easily, fulfilling you both. The two of you are able to express your feelings very easily and this is extremely important for any committed relationship.

If you team up with an Aquarian born between the 9th and the 19th of February, Venus, which is your ruling planet, has a strong affinity with these people. They are romantics at heart and they will easily draw you to them on every level of your being. This could even be one of those romances made in heaven.

LIBRA + PISCES
Air + Water = Rain

Libra and Pisces will quite likely get off to a good start in a relationship, but sustaining your passion is another matter. You're very different people at heart and therefore an extra amount of understanding is going to be essential if you want to overcome your initial hurdles.

For you, Libra, the sensitive and compassionate gestures of Pisces will encourage you in your love for them, but Pisces can also confuse you in that they don't always use their brains to come to a decision or make choices in their lives. If you try to impose your intellectual standards on them, it could create a major stumbling block for you.

On the contrary, you need to operate from an intuitive level when dealing with Pisces. Try to trust your instincts, and let them do the same. Communicating with unspoken words is something that Pisces appreciates. Doing this will help the relationship in many ways. You might not understand it at first, but in due course you will come to realise it is a boon to your partnership.

There are times when Pisces seems to be off with the fairies, completely separate from their surroundings. They need time alone to connect with the forces of nature and to tune into their own spiritual and psychic powers. You need to afford them some opportunities to do that. Once you do, you'll realise this is their way of recharging their batteries, to make them more comfortable in themselves and therefore better at dealing with their day-to-day relationships.

Many Pisceans share their love in an unconditional way, which is something you'll be most surprised about. It is of course rare to find someone who will love you simply for who you are without expecting too much in return. Enjoy this to the fullest; but I need to stress, you must never take advantage of this aspect of Pisces. Reciprocating their love will help grow your relationship.

Individuals born under Pisces between the 20th and the 28th or 29th of February are unusual people who don't fit into normal societal structures. You may find it difficult getting them to join in with your social networks and what you feel is essential for a smooth-functioning life. A lot of give and take will be necessary to make this relationship work.

With Pisces born between the 1st and the 10th of March, a professional connection is excellent for you. Any business you conduct with them will be beneficial and Pisces will serve you so that you can meet your goals and deadlines in a timely manner. Although this relationship is skewed to a financial, professional working relationship, there's always hope that it can develop emotionally and romantically.

A relationship with Pisces born between the 11th and the 20th of March is fantastic! These people are truly soulful, nurturing and compassionate individuals who can help you tune into that part of your being which also loves unconditionally. Your involvement with them will help you recognise the reason you were born.

2010:
The Year Ahead

If you don't know where you are going, any road will get you there.

—Lewis Carroll

Romance and friendship

This is an extraordinarily important year for you, Libra. The year 2010 will bring you to a new level of understanding, both of yourself and your most important relationships. With Saturn, your most powerful planet by birth, being in your Sun sign as the year commences, you are serious about making inroads to your social life, domestic relationships and marital affairs as well.

It will be extremely important to create harmony on the home front, thus giving you a better shot at inner peace, which is the most important component of any relationship. Once you gain equanimity and inner contentment, you realise that everything in your life is destined to be much better.

In January, the interplay of the Sun and Saturn signifies additional responsibilities arising in your family, which in turn will make it difficult for you to enjoy your social life. But this should only last until the middle of January when things should start to improve.

With Venus also trekking through your domestic sphere, you are likely to spend a lot more time giving attention to your living space and your personal relationships with parents, siblings and other relatives. This may be borne out of a sense of obligation or possibly even guilt if previously you haven't had enough time to dedicate to them.

February is Valentine's month and, with Mercury—the exciting, quick-witted and communicative planet—transiting your zone of romance, you could expect this month to be full of life and fun, especially if you are single. With Venus also adding its own touch of good fortune after the 11th, your sense of love, beauty and creativity is heightened. Not only will you attract someone of a good nature but they may be really good looking, too!

Difficulties with friendships arise in February and may not be resolved until the middle of the year. This is due to the influence of Mars in your zone of friendships. You may have heated exchanges with those who are now no longer on the same wavelength as you. You need to remove these adverse influences from your life.

This year is very much about finding peace and creating harmony with people who understand you. If you're finding the going tough, it could be that you've outgrown these relationships and you should be prepared to move on and accept what life offers you graciously.

March is a feel-good month with Jupiter influencing the Sun in a most amazing way. You could receive favourable news that may come from several different directions at once. Friends and lovers will be encouraging and your spiritual insights into human nature will seem to support you.

This is the time of the year when solutions to life's problems can arise from within your own heart. You could be a little over optimistic, however, so don't go promising too much to too many people because you may not be able to fulfil all these obligations.

March is also a good time for those looking to solidify their marriage or long-term, committed relationships. With Venus trekking through your marital sector, your feelings will be easily understood and you can connect deeply with the one you love. Apart from this, you'll be feeling amorous and passionate as well.

You will feel extremely dispersed in April, with your attention flying off in many different directions. Allowing some time to yourself might not be that easy if other commitments are tugging at your heartstrings.

Your passion quotient will increase with Venus in your zone of sexuality, but will you actually have time to make that a reality?

If you happen to be single and you meet someone this month—which is quite likely—try not to make a dash for the finishing line for fear you won't have enough time to spend with the newcomer. It's on the cards that you'll be impulsive, passionate—or should I say, lustful—but might ignore some of the more important ingredients of a relationship. You may therefore overlook some critical character flaws in a stranger and later regret some of your behaviour.

You gain a deeper understanding of life in general from May onwards. Your ruling planet Venus moves through the upper part of your horoscope and thus a good period in 2010 should commence at this time. Mind you, you still have to deal with the ominous overtones of Saturn hovering in Virgo and then later returning to your Sun sign. Fortunately, the philosophical implications of Venus mean you'll be able to go back over your past and carefully assess where you've previously gone wrong and, without too much self-judgement, set things aright. If you've had long-standing grievances with someone, perhaps a friend or relative, this is a good time to bury the hatchet together and move on.

May and June are excellent months to travel, seek out new friendships and alliances through educational pursuits, take on new career objectives, and generally feel great in yourself. These months bring with them a heightened level of self-esteem, which will be noticeable to your friends.

June is also a significant month in that Jupiter will transit into your marital and public relationships sector. With the exciting, abrupt but sometimes unexpected Uranus around, too, expect your life to heat up and bring you some rather dazzling times!

You may want to take a gamble on your relationships throughout July, and Venus will present you with ample opportunities to do so. Your connection with friends and acquaintances will increase; perhaps even overwhelm you at this time. Try to keep calm and don't let your heart run away with your head. You need to look more carefully at others' motivations and your own as well so that you don't put the wrong foot forward.

Mars and Saturn combine their forces in August, which will not be easy for you. The simple solution during this period of the year is not to place too much emphasis on the faults of others. These two planets bring with them much frustration, obstruction and a sense that no one's listening! Perhaps you should remain silent for a while.

Watch your health; don't rush around too much. If you feel as if there are some problems, you should take yourself to get a check-up to gain some peace of mind. You may be overexerting yourself, taking things too seriously and generally doing more than you should. Try to delegate some of these duties to other family members so that the load is distributed fairly.

In the latter part of August, the return of Venus to your Sun sign is a welcome relief from the heavy and sometimes dark energies of Saturn and Mars. With this comes a renewed sense of self-confidence and an ability to express yourself in a more harmonious way. You won't be projecting negative feelings on others and will be able to receive what they have to say as constructive, even if it may not be all that flattering.

September is an excellent time to get a makeover; just go out and buy some new clothes or simply have a good time and splurge on yourself. There's nothing like a bit of 'shopping therapy', is there?

In October, some of your relationships may feel as though they're grinding to a halt. You may wonder if your popularity is declining. After the previous month of such great highs, it's understandable that you might feel some let down, especially if others have been distracted by new interests and possibly new relationships. You mustn't take this personally.

On the home front, everything might seem a little boring. It's up to you to use your imagination and positive energy to change things.

The presence of Venus and Mars indicates there is a great deal of passion within you, but you might not be able to find an adequate outlet for such energy this month.

In November, with Mars's entrance into Sagittarius, your zone of short journeys, you'll be feeling much perkier. Get out and about, take some short trips, visit a museum or go on a boat trip—anything to get out—and this will clear your mind and give you a brand new lease on life.

With the Moon commencing its transit in your twelfth zone of secrets, hidden enemies, hospitals and asylums, there may be issues surrounding a friend's mental or physical wellbeing and you may need to help them. This is a month when your compassion will be spotlighted.

In December, constructive discussions will draw the year to a neat close. Re-asserting your commitment to friends and lovers, gaining a deeper understanding and getting them to commit to their part of the relationship, will be important as 2010 comes to an end. Use your powers of persuasion to get others 'to cut you a fairer deal' in love. If your emotional, sexual or spiritual needs haven't been fulfilled, it's still not too late to ask for those needs to be met. By doing so, you won't be short-changed and your ideal of peace and harmony for 2010 will be achieved, Libra.

Work and money

You will exhibit considerable emotional energy throughout 2010 and much of this will be projected into your working life.

If for some reason you've been working in a job simply for the sake of earning money, that may all end this year. Your career planet, the Moon, is near fullness when the year commences in January. This is an excellent omen for Librans and you should therefore be confident that your professional life should get off to a good start. But this can only be the case if you put service, creativity and the love of your job before the earnings you hope to make.

Many Librans will be looking to supplement their income and this is shown by Pluto, Venus, the Sun and Mercury influencing the Moon in January. You have an abundance of ideas and by February may be prepared to take a chance on implementing some changes.

Your ruling planet Venus moves into a powerful conjunction with Neptune during February. Your ideals will combine well with your imagination to spur you on to bigger and better things.

What you earn is highlighted by Mars in your zone of profits throughout much of the first half of the year. As I said earlier, you may be aggressively going after additional income without first gaining the respect of others. Reverse the equation. Prove that you are excellent at what you do, give impeccable service, and focus on doing the best job you can. I can assure you that these traits, these characteristics of your personality, when associated with your working life, will bring you the profits you aspire to.

There may be frustrations associated with your professional life due to the powerful influence of Saturn, not just on your work, but on those for whom you work. With the tightening of economies around the world, managers will be placed under immense pressure and could be passing this on to their subordinates. If you're working under someone who's a hard taskmaster, you'll have your work cut out for you and your responsibilities and obligations may increase during this phase of the year. That will continue up until the end of May, because Venus brings you some relief when it enters your zone of work. To some Librans, a new employer, a new boss or a complete change of co-workers will lift your spirits. In some other cases, you could be the one that receives an accolade, a promotion or possibly even a completely new job. Why not? If you need a change, go for it.

Profits, additional cash, gifts, dividends and other unexpected forms of income could be your lot after July. This is an excellent period to enjoy surplus cash but at the same time to splurge on others and share the benefits of these extraordinary life gifts.

You could be overworking in August and September. Take note of your body signals and if you're tired, rest. Supplement your diet with extra vitamins and minerals. You need to make sure that your health isn't jeopardised because this will impact upon your work over the long term.

The period of August and September is very favourable if you're in the business of dealing with the public or working on new business partnerships. Jupiter and Uranus bring considerable luck in this arena. If you're in sales, this combination is likely to result in some brand new clients who will easily come around to your way of thinking and sign off on several big orders. This is a great time for extra commissions due to the Sun moving through Leo, in your zone of profits.

You're able to direct your energies very judiciously in September and October and, far from the Sun and Saturn combination holding you back, the Mars and Venus duo will lift your physical and mental abilities so that some real successes can be achieved. There is a great deal of attention likely to be given to your earnings, your salary, taxes and other financial matters in October when Venus and Mars conjoin. You'll have the support of your employers and in particular some woman who may be an expert in these areas.

Money continues to be a source of pleasure for you in November with the Sun, Venus and Mercury activating that part of your horoscope. Contracts at this time need not be a battle of wills; you can simply listen to another person's viewpoint before stomping on them. You may not be completely happy with the fine print, but if you listen a little more carefully, you'll see that what's on offer may, in fact, create a win–win situation.

You may finish the year with the thought that real estate is possibly a way for you to earn some extra dollars. By all means, investigate what's on offer but don't be too impulsive. There's no rush. With it being Christmas and all, you've probably got other expenses on your mind and the purchase of property or other additional renovations can be deferred until the new year.

Karma, luck and meditation

Your karmic planets are Saturn and Mercury. They endow you with considerable power so your karma will come back abundantly in a positive way during the next twelve months.

You mustn't believe that good karma always feels good. You may have to make some painful decisions in the first three months of the year and once you're able to do this, through the courage of your convictions, you will feel much more peaceful and in control of your life.

Saturn will be stressful only for those Librans who are not prepared to accept that a particular relationship is now ready to be transcended. It's time to move on and, to the extent that you can do this, the universe will then bring you additional, more satisfying opportunities.

In March, when Venus, Uranus, the Sun, Jupiter and Mercury congregate in your sixth zone of work, good luck is likely to occur. This period is also strongly connected to issues of health and vitality. By understanding your body's signals, your heart's desire and your best talents, and then combining them, you will be fortunate in your working life.

One of the best periods of the year for good luck occurs in June and July when Jupiter activates your marital zone. Marriage, long-term commitments and other important personal relationships are highlighted. Jupiter may bless you with a chance meeting or an introduction to someone who is quite likely your soulmate.

Mercury conjoins with Saturn in October. This heralds a period of good fortune for you. There is an added ability to communicate and clearly express yourself. Others will see you as a wiser person with something to contribute. In some philosophies and ancient traditions, the greatest wealth is considered to be knowledge. If that's the case, Libra, the latter part of 2010 should be a wealthy period for you, indeed.

2010:

Month By Month
Predictions

If death meant just leaving the stage long enough to change costume and come back as a new character...
Would you slow down? Or speed up?

—Chuck Palahniuk

Highlights of the month

You demand the best from yourself this year and in January you'll be working hard towards creating harmony in yourself and with those around you. There is an extraordinarily powerful amount of energy in the area of home and creativity; therefore, you can expect these parts of your life to be dominant, at least in the first part of January.

After the 3rd, love and friendship combine to give you a great amount of enjoyment and happiness. You'll be trying to accept yourself and others for who they are. Due to the combination of Venus and the Sun, you will be attractive and physically very appealing.

During this time of the year, put forward your best thoughts and creative concepts because you are artistic and will be well received in any sort of cultural endeavour.

There is a great deal of activity in your life and everything seems to be pointing to an intensification between the 13th and the 15th. During this period, Saturn, one of your best karmic planets, moves into its retrogression and shows that you'll be considering things past. In your relationships, you'll be trying to make heads or tails of how you can improve the situation, especially if previously the going has been tough.

If you need to communicate and get things out into the open, do so after the 16th when Mercury, the planet of communication, goes forward in motion. In fact, if you're lazy and postpone things, you could end up finding yourself in a confusing mess, trying to make sense of what others are saying.

Between the 18th and the 25th, you'll notice a big change in your work routine. Your diary planning and any sort of schedule that is going to impact upon you and your family will need to be ironed out very, very clearly. If you've been planning a strategy, it's time now to put that into practice. This could involve dietary changes, an exercise program at the gym, or some new schedule in the workplace.

You must remember that no one is an island unto themselves and, therefore, collaborative work with your colleagues will be important to achieve what you want.

January will also be important for Libran-born individuals because for you, your new year's resolution this year will be more important than ever before. It's time to turn over a new leaf.

After the 20th, children will become the focus of your attention, especially creatively. You'll be working with them to help them identify aspects of their personalities that can best make them happy. You can join in with the fun and games or perhaps join forces to involve yourself in a creative pursuit that they're thinking of trying, too. You might just discover that this is something you're interested in as well.

If you burn the candle at both ends, it might be time to pull back. Your health may be a problem after the 25th, so take note of your body signals and get adequate rest.

Romance and friendship

Meeting people and generally getting out and about, connecting with new acquaintances and searching for new romantic partners is very well favoured between the 1st and the 4th. Because your heart is extremely open, you'll find that the people you meet are extremely receptive and more than willing to give you a chance. Companionship and affection is very much on the cards.

You may want the attention of your spouse or lover on the 5th but may not feel all that comfortable about the way in which they are expressing themselves. To make your relationship harmonious and happier, you may simply have to accept a little less and be sensitive to the needs of your partner.

The period of the 6th to the 10th could be rather frustrating for you and your romantic ambitions may not go all that smoothly. You may have to reconsider your position seriously and take a closer look at your goals and aspirations. Yes, take a long, hard look at what you want and whether or not you've been short-changing yourself so far.

Family affairs are strongly spotlighted between the 11th and the 13th. You may want everything to run like clockwork but, when it doesn't, you'll over-react and could decide that you're simply going to bail out. This is no time for tantrums; try talking and expressing yourself in clearer terms and with more understanding.

Venus moves to your fifth house on the 18th and this is an excellent time to involve yourself in an intense relationship. Your creative impulses are also strong, so make sure you've factored in some downtime when you can enjoy creative, artistic pursuits in the company of those who have similar interests.

The 20th to the 27th are important days for highlighting and rectifying problems in your relationships. You can try some new psychological techniques on your partner with some good effects.

Your spiritual aspirations need to be checked after the 25th because you're probably dealing with people who are a little out of sync with what your life ambitions are.

Work and money

Between the 1st and the 4th, your working life needn't be difficult as long as you're prepared to go with the flow and adjust by making the appropriate changes to your workplace. This is going to take some flexibility on your part.

Additional changes, some of them major, should also take place around the 8th. Be careful that this doesn't upset the applecart of your life as a whole, because any sort of impulsive move could have a strong bearing on the stability of your income.

Between the 15th and the 18th, you could be prone to bouts of irritability and may say and do things to your co-workers that will leave you feeling regretful. Don't hurry your decisions and, if you're angry, get out of your workplace so that you don't create even more difficulties for yourself.

After the 23rd, you're likely to be prone to some sort of accident or injury. This is a continuation of the previous prediction where you must take your time and not ignore any safety precautions for the sake of getting to your destination quickly.

Between the 27th and the 30th, you'll need to be a little stubborn if you're going to get your own way. Stand your ground and, even if confronted by authority figures, don't budge. You are correct in your assessments and will be so proven.

Destiny dates

Positive: 1, 2, 3, 4, 13, 14, 26
Negative: 5, 6, 7, 8, 9, 10, 11, 12, 15, 16, 17
Mixed: 18, 19, 20, 21, 22, 23, 24, 25, 27, 28, 29, 30

Highlights of the month

It could be easy to idealise love in February, particularly between the 1st and the 8th. Why is this? Because Saturn may be demanding so many responsibilities of you that you need a way out. Be careful, however, because you're likely to assume much more of a relationship than is actually there. This will be more important for singles who are out there clubbing, meeting others and feeling as if the person they meet at this time is Mr or Miss Perfect. It just isn't so. Remember to keep your wits about you and remind yourself that we're all human and therefore possess frailties.

Between the 10th and the 14th, you have some brilliant ideas that you can act upon. However, Mars being in your zone of friendships may not allow you to share these ideas as comfortably as you would like. It could be that there's some opposition within your peer group and that general tension will make you feel uncomfortable. Just remember it's not absolutely necessary to share every bit of information with those you normally hang out with. Test the water first and don't be too outlandish in what you're proposing.

Quite a few planetary forces converge on your workplace around the 15th and this continues until around the 18th. What this means is that you'll be carefully analysing how you can improve your financial and mental conditions with respect to your working life.

The Sun also conjoins the zone of work and health on the 18th of February, which indicates a critical time for you or someone close to you as far as their health is concerned. There's no point working yourself into the ground for the sake of money if you're not feeling well. Remember that there is little else as important as your health.

You aspire to some new philosophical viewpoints between the 27th and the 28th. You may be thinking deeply about the meaning of life and how you can improve your understanding of things. Psychology, spirituality and other self-analytical activities will be of great interest to you and may be helpful in clarifying your purpose during this stage of your life.

Romance and friendship

Women feature strongly in your life after the 2nd. You need to make communicating a priority, especially if you feel that you've neglected someone; for example, your mother, an aunt or a grandmother.

These transits will reach a peak sometime around the 9th when family matters will intensify and you'll have to bite the bullet and put aside an appropriate amount of time to satisfy these people in your life.

Between the 10th and the 14th, you are extremely amorous so take full advantage of it. If you find yourself in the wrong company, you've only got yourself to blame. Think carefully before making appointments with those whom you don't find particularly interesting. You've got quite a few people to choose from, so why settle for second best?

Passions are strong around the 19th; with your feelings running hot, your instincts and your deeper emotions are likely to dominate and control your mind. This will satisfy your body but you may have some feelings of regret the morning after.

Sport, travel and other intellectual pursuits all indicate an exciting time between the 21st and the 26th. Pencil in a few social engagements to your diary and don't forget that, if the concert is not particularly your cup of tea, you can still have a good night out with your friends.

You could be jealous, angry or simply operating from a base of fear when you react to a certain situation or statements that are made around the 27th. Don't stir up trouble where a more passive attitude will help smooth things over. You're responsible for the outcome of the situation at this time.

Time out with your loved one on the 28th is an excellent idea. Not only romance but a nurturing energy will envelop you and the one you love. This period is great for a weekend away and provides an opportunity for you to forget the stressful worries of day-to-day life for a while.

Work and money

Don't burn your bridges too quickly, even if you feel completely dissatisfied with where you're at in your working life. Between the 2nd and the 8th, you could be feeling as if you're treading water and not getting anywhere. You may also sense that you're not getting the respect you should be. This is a passing phase so don't act on a knee jerk reaction.

Business agreements or other verbal interactions could grind to a halt and be very frustrating sometime around the 14th. You need to read between the lines and not be too quick to assume that everything on offer is in your best interests.

Your confidence and your physical energy as well are in top gear by the 17th. Moreover, Venus conjoins Jupiter in your zone of work, indicating some lucky opportunities. Is this luck, or perhaps the wonderful, vibrant energy that you're giving off, which is attracting those opportunities to you in the first place? Probably the latter.

Between the 26th and the 28th, be careful not to allow your personal relationships to interfere with the smooth functioning of your work. Telephone calls and other distracting pieces of information of a personal nature may not be looked upon too favourably by your employers.

Destiny dates

Positive: 15, 16, 17, 21, 22, 23, 24, 25

Negative: 18

Mixed: 1, 2, 3, 4, 5, 6, 7, 8, 9, 10, 11, 12, 13, 14, 19, 26, 27, 28

Highlights of the month

Saturn and Uranus present you with a seesaw of emotional activity throughout the month of March. Not only that, Venus conjoins Uranus in its transit on the 4th, which reflects a need for change, excitement and the unknown. With Venus also moving into a favourable aspect to Mars, your passions will run high and it's likely you'll be daring enough to try something different in terms of your relationships.

If you're with a partner who's open to change and possibly even something a little strange, this could be a very interesting time. On the other hand, if you're in partnership with someone, or are friends with more conservative characters, you will need to break free and put your stamp of originality on your life and its events during this month.

Mars ploughs forward in its transit on the 10th and again, while remaining in your zone of friendships, shows clearly that these first few months of 2010 will be strongly focused on clearing up your relationships in this area of life. Siblings are also included under the heading of Mars and the eleventh zone of your horoscope, which indicates a need to reconnect with long-lost brothers and sisters or to clarify your position with them if there've been some misunderstandings. The fact that Mars is moving forwards is a good omen and should bring some positive results and a closeness that may not have been there for some time.

Communicate your ideas forcefully, particularly in business, from the 15th. Your originality will win the day. Make sure, however, you have some spare time up your sleeve because older members of your family, employers and other authority figures may throw you a curved ball that will result in a change of plans. This could affect the rest of the month if you're not prepared.

Excellent communications take place between you and your partner between the 17th and the 20th. Mercury's transit through your zone of marriage and public relations makes you popular, witty and able to explain lucidly how you feel. However, try not to be too clever with what you have to say, otherwise it might sound as if you're speaking from the head rather than the heart. Of course, you want others to believe you, so may I suggest you talk about how you *feel*, rather than what you *think*?

Venus gives you a great deal of sensuality on the 31st, which continues into April. You'll actively want to explore the deeper facets of your relationship.

Romance and friendship

After the 1st, you may be feeling a little low-key because of an infatuation with someone that can't be fulfilled. Patience is a virtue, as they say, but you may have to wait a little longer than you think to fulfil these romantic ambitions.

You'll be meeting people who can benefit you in many aspects of life, not just socially, on the 7th. You'll be learning a lot about yourself and can expand your mind to take an interest in many new topics that are introduced to you by these people.

Around the 10th, you may find yourself in a personal encounter that is quite powerful. This can be for either good or bad, depending on how you react to the person in question. In any case, it will be a memorable event that should open new doorways of self-understanding.

Try to think in terms of a team spirit between the 18th and the 25th. You may want to be independent and that's okay; but others may see you as being somewhat selfish if you don't open your heart and take part in the group mentality. Once you show that you're a team player, you'll have ample support for doing things your way.

By the 26th, you'll be more prepared to seek the association of others and not do things too much by yourself. There's a collaborative spirit of enterprise and a cycle in which you'll support your spouse or lover in some endeavour or enterprise.

Between the 29th and 31st, if you find yourself

in some type of emotional difficulty, you mustn't feel embarrassed. It could be the perfect time to seek out the advice of a professional counsellor or consultant.

Work and money

It's likely you'll really want to thrash yourself this month. Remember, it's not necessary to push yourself into the ground. The period of the 1st to the 4th is particularly notable for this very reason. You may not realise until after the damage is done that you've been putting in too many hours and really not treating yourself with kindness. You can get the job done without running yourself into the ground.

Have you made the wrong decision and pursued a professional path that is just not in keeping with who you are? You may discover the stark reality of this fact between the 6th and the 9th and it's up to you to admit you're not travelling the path that is designed to bring out your best colours. Make a change, get out of what you're doing, or at least investigate the alternatives.

You could invest in some artistic objects, furnishings or antiques after the 17th. Such investments show that the activity is not only a dry, mathematical enterprise. This is perfect for your Libran temperament because you do need to connect with things of beauty. Here's your chance to combine money-making with the aesthetic side of your personality.

Travel and work are linked very powerfully between the 21st and the 25th and, by accepting a commission to journey away, even if initially it seems inconvenient, it will bring you some good financial rewards.

Destiny dates

Positive: 7, 15, 17, 18, 19, 20, 21, 22, 23, 24, 25, 26
Negative: 29, 30
Mixed: 1, 2, 3, 4, 6, 7, 8, 9, 10, 31

Highlights of the month

You're seeing things in much more detail this month, which is due to the placement of Mercury in the most mysterious zone of your horoscope. Throughout the period of the 2nd until the 7th you will be penetrating in your understanding and will want a deeper, more meaningful relationship. Anything superficial will not satisfy you.

Strangely, you will see that many of your friendships are not based on deep or lasting principles, and because of this you will take a grim view of the habitual sorts of friendships that have simply been connections of convenience. This is the time for you to weed out those people who are no longer of any use to you and seek out characters who have more to offer.

During the same period, Pluto goes retrograde, and Saturn, too, in its backward motion, moves into your most secretive zone, indicating that you'll be dealing with many of your own psychological complexes. Issues from your past or unresolved problems with parents and other relatives will be highlighted and have to be dealt with.

This is an excellent time to enter into spiritual and meditative practices for the purpose of clearing your mind and your subconscious. Your dreams will be powerful, maybe even 'premonitional'. Your intuitive sense will be an impeccable guide to what needs to be removed from your life and what needs to remain. Trust this implicitly.

Financial issues will attract your attention after the 18th. You need to get clear on what your position is in business, especially if you happen to be an independent business operator, running your own company or enterprise, and more so if you have others in partnership with you. There may be some dissatisfaction about the way your money is being handled. We can extend this idea to banks, account-ants, investment portfolios, stocks and shares. You may be feeling uncomfortable about how your money is being managed by any or all of these people or institutions.

If you think about it carefully, you'll realise you've probably been a little lazy in doing your homework and gaining a broader understanding of your financial circumstances. By relying on others, you've been left in the dark. It's time to turn on your light of knowledge.

A less serious, even funny, cycle is likely after the 25th. Venus brings with it pleasant learning experiences, educational pursuits and possibly even long journeys. Your connections with foreigners and those at a distance will also be spotlighted and romance can blossom away from home.

When the Sun conjoins Mercury in your zone of joint finances on the 28th, you may have to revisit some of the earlier points I was making. In other words, make sure you have a good lawyer, even if a little expensive, if there is a contentious issue looming.

Romance and friendship

Sometimes making peace with yourself can create war with others, or inwardly you may be feeling uneasy, even though you're putting on a good front. Between the 1st and the 5th you'll find yourself in situations where you're not particularly comfortable and no one else is any better off for it. Spend time alone if being with others irritates you.

If you don't happen to be feeling well around the 10th, let your family and your loved ones know. You may retaliate, and they may be unaware of the reason for your dramatic mood swings.

Who rules the roost at home? You need to sort that out before Mercury goes retrograde on the 18th. Power struggles could emerge and if you don't resolve them before that date, things could linger for a couple of weeks longer, leaving you in an uncertain limbo. Someone may be unreasonably demanding.

Around the 21st, you may find yourself in the company of people who are a little bit snobbish.

This could leave you feeling less than confident. If something doesn't go as well as you would it like to, you mustn't be unmerciful to your own weaknesses. Forgive yourself; this is essential to developing a greater character.

The period of the 22nd to the 25th is exciting, to say the least. You'll be driven to get away from it all, kick up your heels and really have a shindig of a time. You'll be loud, boisterous, and that's exactly the way you'll want to play it. This is an excellent form of therapy, to release tension.

If you've been procrastinating on changing some of those personal habits that you absolutely detest, it's time to do so around the 28th. Your willpower will be strong and you can be successful if you put your mind to it.

Work and money

The period of the 2nd to the 5th is a great time but you may be resting on your laurels a little too heavily. You need to continue to take full advantage of your current work situation and build upon that for greater success in the future.

You can feel very focused between the 7th and the 9th. Write down what you want and work systematically towards achieving those ends. You'll accomplish a great deal; and not only that, you'll have a bit of fun doing your work as well.

You can avoid a fight with someone on the work front between the 11th and the 15th. The reason for this is that you're able to speak your mind rather than bottling up your feelings and later exploding. Use forethought to consider what sort of consequence is likely by saying something.

Reconsider your contracts or any sort of agreement between the 16th and the 19th. Don't cut corners and, if need be, stay up a little later to go through everything with a fine-tooth comb to get the maximum benefit for yourself. Someone in authority could offer you a new opportunity around the 23rd.

You'll be extremely hectic between the 26th and the 27th. Stress is the likely result, but because it is self-imposed, you'll eventually work it out.

Destiny dates

Positive: 6, 7, 8, 9, 16, 17, 19, 22, 23, 24, 25

Negative: 10, 18, 21, 26, 27

Mixed: 1, 5, 11, 12, 13, 14, 15, 18, 28

Highlights of the month

This month you need to establish the real motive for why you are helping others. It's quite likely you've put considerable effort into assisting someone achieve their dreams, only to find that you've eroded your time by not getting much back in return. Did you do this to gain something for yourself, or were you genuinely unconditional in your love and support?

Between the 1st and the 5th, your attention will be on the success of others; but don't worry too much about that because this is a month of the year when you too can finally shine in all your professional glory.

Venus enters your most powerful zone of career on the 20th, and all of your attention will be on this area of your life. Not only that, all eyes will be on you! Your popularity should be stunning, to say the least. You'll be attractive, graceful and very persuasive in any arena and can impress your employers very, very easily.

This is the time of the year when a professional promotion is likely. For those of you seeking out new employment, this transit of Venus will most definitely give you the edge against your competitors. Your new employers—or at least those who are interviewing you, such as employment agencies and so forth— will find you very appealing and so much so they will recommend you for the position you seek.

Unexpected events surround your most personal relationships after the 28th. Uranus, the planet of dynamic and electric energy, will visit your marital zone. It's hard to tell how this will play out for each individual born under Libra, but let's just say there will never be a dull moment once this planet commences its seven-year cycle in this zone of your horoscope.

This can mean suddenly meeting someone who sweeps you off your feet or, conversely, suddenly walking away from a relationship, even if you thought nothing was particularly wrong with it. There's an element of progressive curiosity associated with this cycle, so the best I can suggest is that you enjoy it and remain open to what life has to offer.

In friendship and family life you may be highly strung this month, so it's best not to do too much and take up only one thing at a time. You're likely to cram your diary and find yourself stressed as a result, even due to fun pastimes such as parties or other social events. Know your limits. Even Clint Eastwood said in *Dirty Harry*, 'A man's got to know his limitations.'

Your search for answers and delving into the past and other nostalgic memories will be fully realised by the 30th, when Saturn again goes direct in its movement. At this time, it's certain you will have uncovered something about yourself that will help you to move forward.

Romance and friendship

On the 2nd, try to sidestep any tense confrontations. Someone will be aching for an argument, but there will be one only if you play by their rules.

Between the 5th and the 8th, your adventurous nature comes to the forefront. You could be impatient, however, and want fun at any cost, without any interruption or objection. If someone in authority is questioning your motives, this could make you angry.

On the 9th, your desire to be personally free of any constraints continues. You'll be demanding your rights in a relationship and again, if you feel that there's opposition to what you feel is fair, you're likely to lash out.

On the 11th, Mercury goes direct so any discussions or opportunities for friendship that may have been delayed are likely to move forward positively. This is a co-operative period where you can share love and friendship in abundant measure.

Between the 14th and the 16th, you feel gentle and tender toward your loved ones. You may even want to do something for them without any thought of return. Your act of kindness now will not be noticed or rewarded, although that may not have been your motivation, anyway.

You feel emotionally supported between the 23rd and the 25th, so take what you can get, I say. Your personal relationships are very much intensified and sexuality is also strong in your relationship. Sex is a powerful form of expression and will make you feel revived.

There may be some interference from outside forces in your personal romantic situation. You mustn't allow others to stick their nose into business that isn't theirs; but then again, you may have invited these opinions. If you've made your bed, so to speak, you've got to sleep in it. You need to tell others clearly if you don't want them to offer their opinions.

Work and money

Between the 7th and the 11th, you may be torn between the demands of your workplace and those of your family. You may want to socialise with those in your professional arena but demands at home may make that difficult. This can make you feel blocked and angry and not as supported as you'd like.

Something has to be sacrificed, if only temporarily, on the 14th. Try to compromise with your friends and your work colleagues.

There's a high level of energy around you on the 18th, but this could quickly turn sour and change from friendly competitiveness to out-and-out war. Lay down the terms of engagement before getting involved and, if you're not a good sport, don't play.

A honeymoon may be over for some Librans around the 24th because you realise that what was supposed to be a beautiful stroll down to the park is now a heavy-duty responsibility. Get real and don't demand that life be something other than it is.

You could become more philosophical and at the same time flexible about your belief systems around the 31st.

Destiny dates

Positive: 1, 2, 3, 4, 5, 6, 15, 16, 20, 23, 25, 31
Negative: 10, 28
Mixed: 7, 8, 9, 11, 14, 24

Highlights of the month

June continues to be an excellent month for your popularity and success in all areas of your life. You must remember, however, that sometimes relying on your good looks, your charm and other social aspects may be a mistake. You mustn't forget to continue to work hard as this will increase your chances for success.

Your luck continues to spill over between the 1st and the 5th. On the 6th, when Jupiter enters the seventh zone of your horoscope, you will connect even more strongly with the public and can attract some very lucky opportunities, indeed.

With the conjoining of Uranus and Jupiter making a very powerful influence on your Sun sign, sudden meetings, either of a professional or personal nature, should be approached with great confidence. You will be the darling of all present and will achieve your ends very easily. Even if there's some opposition to your ideas, you'll easily win over the hearts of others and convince them of your strategy or plan.

Mars exits your zone of friendship on the 7th and indicates a resolution to longstanding difficulties or irritations with your existing peer group. With its transit into your twelfth zone of quietude, secrets and hospitals, there may be a need for you to show your support for a relative or friend during their time of distress. There could be an apparent health problem bothering them and your assistance will greatly relieve them of their suffering.

There is considerable tension mounting in this same area of your horoscope and, coupled with some of the other planetary combinations, my strong recommendation for you is not to take life too lightly and certainly don't take uncalculated risks. In a financial sense, you may want to throw your money into an area that you think will return you with profits very, very quickly and easily. But this rarely happens, so don't be fooled by your own greed.

Another type of gamble is that of a romantic nature. Jumping out of the pan and into the fire simply because you think the grass is greener on the other side will leave you short-changed in the end.

You may have a dilemma concerning your spending habits this month and this is due to the increasing tension between Mars and Saturn in your zone of expenditure. While you realise you need to purchase a gift for someone, you may not financially be in a position to do so. Consider that the thought really does count and that, if you shop wisely, you can buy something that is within your budget and still great.

New friends are on the horizon between the 14th and the 21st and this indicates celebrations, parties and other festive engagements, which are a great deal of fun. This is also the time to extend your circle of influence and attract people from different cultures and interests into your orb. Someone, or several people, you meet during this phase of the year will excite you with their different ideas. This is a time of learning and growth socially.

An unexpected opportunity arises in your workplace between the 22nd and the 30th. You may be offered an interim position that involves some authority but also some additional responsibility.

Romance and friendship

You mustn't allow a fear of change to stop you from experiencing life to the fullest between the 1st and the 6th. If you get stuck in a dogmatic way of viewing things, your attitude will never allow you to grow and become the person you are destined to become.

When Mars moves to your twelfth zone of quietude on the 7th, your emotional, physical and mental drive may be lowered and you may be susceptible to illness. Your immune system may be depleted, so take such precautions as dietary supplements and extra rest while keeping your feelings light and breezy.

If some of your dreams and hopes of a romantic nature haven't been realised yet, you have a chance to reaffirm what you want on the 8th and the 9th. At the same time, keep in mind you should direct your energies into a fruitful pursuit rather than wasting your valuable love on someone who couldn't care less.

Disciplining your feelings is what's required between the 14th and the 15th. You have to work on your self-control. Any tangles in your love life can be set straight through purposefulness on your part.

Your sexual drive is very strong on the 17th, but don't forget that you need to satisfy your partner, too, not just yourself. Remember that marriage and/or a deeply committed relationship is a two-way street.

There's a high degree of tension in your relationships between the 19th and 24th. In fact, you may be attracting people who are not at all what you superficially see them to be. You'll be shocked at their responses and will realise you need to spend a little more time understanding human nature before making snap judgements.

Between the 28th and the 30th, you should try hard not to seek others' approval for who you are. By defining yourself through other people's eyes, you do yourself a great disservice. Dig deep and feel good in yourself for who you are, not what others expect you to be.

Work and money

You're trying to the see the best in yourself and others between the 4th and the 8th, which can be expressed through your work. If you're not completely satisfied with what you're doing, make a new plan and seek the advice of others to help you. You don't necessarily have to leave the job you're in; a shift sideways may be just as advantageous.

On the 10th, witnessing a misuse of power could bother you. You can see that someone is manipulating the group but at the same time may be ill-equipped and not in a position to do anything about it. Think more deeply about how to deal with it because you can't allow tyranny to dominate good people.

On the 13th and 14th you'll be feeling extremely confident in your work and realise you have the opportunity to create some new seeds of growth. Forget about your past mistakes; at least, learn from them but don't dwell upon them.

Between the 26th and the 28th, the lunar eclipse means that the seeds of change are indeed being sown and it could be the perfect time to step forward into a change of work and lifestyle. This must be preceded by some sort of self-improvement plan, psychological self-assessment or educational course.

Destiny dates

Positive: 4, 5, 6, 13, 14, 15, 16, 17, 18, 25, 26, 27, 28, 29, 30

Negative: 9, 10

Mixed: 7, 8, 19, 20, 21, 22, 23, 24

Highlights of the month

Individuality will be extremely important to you this month. With the Sun and Mercury conjoining in the most important sector of the zodiac for you, you want to make a lasting impression on others and, between the 3rd and the 7th, you can do so. Try not to become obsessive about how you look and what others think of you, however, because this might come across as fake. Just be yourself and let the energies of the cosmos do their thing for you.

With Mars still continuing its trek through your twelfth zone of the past, you mustn't let what's happened in yesteryear dominate your feelings. There could be reminders of unpleasant experiences through bumping into people who were part of those experiences. It could be uncomfortable, letting go of these events and treating people for who they are now without any past judgements. This might be a big lesson for you.

Between the 9th and 11th, friendships feature very strongly. Venus moves through your area of social life and important karmic relationships, bringing new prospects for you to seek out exciting adventures. This is also an excellent time to meet and develop a deep and meaningful relationship with someone important. This is also highlighted by Jupiter and Uranus in your marital zone.

The solar eclipse which occurs on the 11th has deep and lasting ramifications for your professional life. Keep in mind that, with the power you achieve now, additional responsibilities will have to be shouldered as well, so try to educate yourself and associate with others who are prepared to deal with you on a mutual professional level. Your successes now could cause others to take a swipe at you and this may be done in a very covert way. Hold your head up and don't be drawn into petty arguments.

Between the 17th and the 20th, your feelings and actions are completely synchronised and, therefore, fewer distractions will bother you. It's likely you'll be quite reactive if others aren't on your wavelength and so patience may be in short supply. Harness your energy in a constructive manner rather than wasting it and, by the 23rd, you'll be amazed at how much you can actually achieve.

You'll realise your spending habits need to be curtailed and this will bother you, especially if you've had your heart set on purchasing one or two luxury items. Discipline will be the key to success this month, which intensifies as Mars and Saturn get more deeply involved with each other in the heavens.

Your vibes will be totally positive after the 29th and, with Mars entering your Sun sign, you'll be up-beat and confident, so don't hang around too many emotional cripples because you're going to realise very quickly that the company you keep will determine whether or not you're able to maintain this good state of mind.

Romance and friendship

Between the 2nd and the 4th it will be easy for you to become overenthusiastic and overconfident in a complete overestimation of someone. You may go overboard and squander your emotional assets. Don't exaggerate the benefits that someone offers you, nor their personality.

Between the 6th and the 8th, you could feel as if it's okay to act out of character, almost strangely, and this could be a psychological method of distancing yourself from others. You'll also be attracted to people who are exotic and who don't follow the normal patterns of society. You could find yourself dealing with unusual people.

The 11th is an excellent time to travel and venture away from your normal haunts. Your desire to create a new circle of friends is strong. From the 14th to the 18th, new friendships and romances are likely to emerge, even out of nowhere. Your current relationships can be revitalised.

You can enhance your personal appearance and look your best between the 17th and the 20th. Get out and purchase some new clothes; arrange for a new hairstyle or even change the colour of your hair to make a social statement.

Between the 26th and the 28th, you may need to withdraw your energies from your peer group or family. Someone may not understand why you're doing this and could be even more demanding, which will get your back up. You need to let them know in no uncertain terms that respect is the first and foremost foundation of friendship.

You'll start to see cracks forming in the friendships you've held dear for sometime between the 29th and the 31st. You can see the flaws and problems associated with some of your long-term friends and need to do something about it. You'll feel especially exhausted by this and need time out.

Work and money

You don't always have to be running hither and thither to get things done. The period of the 7th to the 10th is an excellent time to reflect quietly on where you are at on your path and how things are going professionally. Collect your thoughts.

Your workplace activities could be thrown into a tailspin so expect the unexpected between the 17th and the 20th. Those calling the shots may not really have a clear-cut idea of what they want and where they're going, so it's up to you to help them make those decisions.

Plan more effectively in terms of your long-range ambitions on the 28th. What you aspire to in your career can become clearly focused, so these issues are spotlighted in the last few days of the month.

Expect some recognition for your good work because your employers will support you in it around the 31st. A coveted position could come your way, which will be cause for celebration.

For those of you who are more independent by nature, it's a good idea to take the initiative and don't wait around for others to mollycoddle you. If you rely too much on what others are going to do or say, you could be waiting around forever. No, it's up to you to go grab some success for yourself!

Destiny dates

Positive: 9, 10, 11, 23

Negative: 2, 26, 27

Mixed: 3, 4, 5, 6, 7, 8, 17, 18, 19, 20, 28, 29, 31

Highlights of the month

You won't mind getting your hands dirty this month, Libra, and that's to be expected due to the conjoining of Mars and Saturn in your Sun sign. In fact, I might go so far as to say that unless you get down and do some hard physical work, you're probably not going to feel that great in yourself.

You'll need to let off steam, so working in the garden, heavy lifting, manual or dextrous work as well as a good workout or two in the gym will be just what the doctor ordered. If you push yourself hard between the 1st and the 6th, you'll feel much better about yourself. This will act as a sort of clearing out, to allow you to enjoy the rest of the month much more.

Venus enters your Sun sign on the 7th and makes contact with Saturn. Although you'll feel good, you might be in the company of more conservative people. Be careful how you present yourself and don't assume that others are going to think exactly like you. You first need to scout out the territory if you've been invited to a party or some other social gathering just to figure out what people's reactions to you will be like.

Your drive is electric and intense between the 14th and the 20th. You won't be able to sit still and it could be that your sense of initiative and power will be a little too much for those who work with you. Try to pace yourself a little and explain your manoeuvres and objectives to others before you rush headlong into a project. You'll be better able to gain the support of your co-workers by going a little more slowly.

Your larger-than-life expectations could come to a screeching halt sometime around the 21st. Someone whom you trust may not be as trusting of you. This is probably because of your enthusiastic approach. They may feel as though you've got some sort of hidden agenda. You will be a little disappointed that your efforts won't be reciprocated equally.

Relationships are generally not going to be too fulfilling this month and you can put this down to the direct influence of Saturn, Mars and Uranus. Expect tension, miscommunication and a tendency for your partner to react—or rather, overreact—to your suggestions. The period of the 23rd to the 27th is a 'hair-trigger' cycle, which means you need to explain yourself more softly and keep in mind the perspectives of others if you don't want the situation to blow apart.

Re-evaluate your work circumstances through-out August. The position or opportunity you thought would satisfy you deeply could leave you high and dry. You will come to realise that just because you may be earning a little more money, it doesn't necessarily mean you've gained a greater satisfaction from the work itself.

Romance and friendship

It's not a great idea to push your own interests on the 2nd, even though you may be particularly energetic. You may find yourself alienating others, possibly even intimidating them. It's more impor-tant to consider sensitively what these people need rather than what you want. The truth of the matter is that by showing an interest in others, you'll also get what you want in the process. That's the law of karma.

Between the 6th and the 10th, you're extremely passionate and this is a time of sexual revitalisa-tion. Exploring your own, most intimate emotional and physical needs will be important to you. You need to make this clear to your partner or this could be construed as a form of selfishness on your part.

The 14th to the 16th is an excellent time to consider travel and vacationing. Get out the travel brochures and do some serious research on where it is you'd like to go and with whom you'd like to share some precious time away.

Talk about your feelings on the 17th because someone is quite prepared to listen to what you have to say. In fact, you may not realise it but the topic of discussion may be exactly what they need to hear.

There's a theme of sharing that continues through from the 20th to the 23rd, and this could involve your spiritual and philosophical interests. You may be going through an overhaul in terms of your perception of life because of the experiences you've been through and, once again, what you have to say to others will strike a chord in their own hearts.

Adjustments are necessary between the 26th and the 28th. You need to be flexible for the sake of keeping the peace on the home front.

Work and money

You'll probably be overextending yourself between the 8th and the 10th; but by the same token, you'll be focusing on your work and getting rid of the backlog that's been sitting on your desk.

On the 12th, you can tackle any mundane chores and other domestic issues that have been hanging in midair. Enlist the help of other family members to help you get through the mountain of work. A key word at this time is 'delegation'.

Between the 14th and the 18th, you are much less aggressive and become more relaxed about your work.

Between the 20th and the 25th, 'the devil is in the details' but you need to be aware that some of the information you require may not be forthcoming and you'll have to wait for a little longer until you can put these issues—that is, contracts and other agreements—to bed.

On the 28th, you have the ability to articulate your viewpoint clearly but in the process may annoy the hell out of someone else.

Destiny dates

Positive: 6, 7, 14, 15, 16, 17, 18, 19

Negative: 2

Mixed: 8, 9, 10, 20, 21, 22, 23, 24, 25, 26, 27, 28

SEPTEMBER

Highlights of the month

A passionate period commences with Mars and Venus causing you to take the initiative in love. Even if you're a woman, you won't have any problem making the first move or at least letting someone of the opposite sex have a clear insight into your intentions. Make your moves between the 1st and the 6th. This will be favourable for you and the responses you get will be equally passionate.

Your focus is distracted from love and personal affairs between the 9th and the 12th when Jupiter re-enters your zone of work and daily routine. This also is telling on your level of debt. You'll need to make some substantial repayments, not only to feel comfortable but to get ahead. In fact, there may be some letter of demand or an unexpected notification that indicates you've fallen behind and were unaware of the fact.

Contracts, communications and any sort of agreement that you need to clarify or resolve should take place after the 13th when Mercury moves into direct motion. Many of these discussions will be behind the scenes or perhaps even done over the phone or through the Internet. This may make it a little trickier because at least when you're dealing with someone eye to eye, you can see their responses and whether or not what you're saying is having a positive impact. For this reason, you need to take some extra precautions when going through these discussions.

Between the 14th and the 19th, arguments over money are again looming. You may burn a hole in your pocket and overspend. By the same token, you are quite aggressive in making money and could find yourself unconsciously slipping back into the discussion of how much you wish to make, how much you've spent and who has more than who, which might become boring to some of your nearest and dearest. Remain sensitive to what they feel about finances, if indeed they want to discuss these matters at all.

Gaining power could, to you, seem to have a lot to do with how much you earn or what you possess. Your value system may be in for a rude shock if you're measuring who you are by your possessions. Take a longer and harder look at these aspects of your life so that you come to some true conclusions. When the Sun enters your sign of Libra on the 23rd, your expression and sense of power lifts to a new high. This is an excellent time of the year where your confidence and your ability to achieve much more is strongly marked.

Romance and friendship

It's time to make your dreams about love a reality, especially between the 1st and the 3rd. If you're infatuated by someone, you mustn't think that life is going to bring them falling into your lap. Take the appropriate measures to let them know how you feel.

Between the 5th and the 7th, you may be completely incorrect in your assessment of a friend or situation. Try to see things objectively. If domestic disputes seem to be dominating your emotional landscape on the 8th, it's likely that people on the outside have had something to do with it. You need to stop 'airing your dirty laundry', or the 'someone' within the family who is leaking information they shouldn't, needs to be taken to task.

On the 13th and 14th, you must let off steam in ways that are acceptable. Banging your head against a wall is not an acceptable way.

Between the 16th and the 18th, you could be taking out your anger on others and becoming obsessed over some trivial issue. Is it worth all the angst? Let it go if it's not that important.

Women in your life will come to the fore between the 19th and the 24th. You may be surprised to connect with someone who is much older than you but who seems to have many of the answers you're looking for. Develop this relationship because you can learn much about yourself and where you can be in future.

Between the 26th and the 30th, you can initiate a new love affair that will really make you feel good but it mustn't be based upon you babying someone else. This must be a relationship of equality where both your and their needs are met equally.

Work and money

It's quite likely that disagreements based upon your differences of opinion with others in your workplace will occur between the 4th and the 9th. Honesty is certainly a virtue but not if you're too blunt and incapable of taking into account how other people feel. Try to be a little sweeter in your persuasiveness.

Things speed up and you may not be able to keep up with the workload around the 11th. Because you're restless and not as focused as you usually are, you may feel like you're doing a lot but are actually getting nothing done.

From the 16th to the 22nd, make sure you have ample business cards with you if you're working in a commercial environment. You'll be making plenty of new business contacts and these individuals can open doors for you in the future.

Between the 26th and the 30th, you mustn't come on too strongly if you're trying to close a deal. This could scare away a prospective client. With work colleagues, you might be trying forcefully to push your methodologies on them and this will create discomfort for them. If those you work with, or those who work for you, have been doing the job adequately, why try to fix what isn't broken?

Destiny dates

Positive: 1, 2, 3, 20, 21, 22, 23, 24

Negative: 8, 15

Mixed: 4, 5, 6, 7, 9, 10, 11, 12, 13, 14, 16, 17, 18, 19,
26, 27, 28, 29, 30

Highlights of the month

It's a funny thing how we desire success in life, but then, after hard work, when the opportunities are finally presented, we become nervous; become concerned that we're letting go of something that has held us in good stead and is a comfortable space for us. However, that's exactly what may happen throughout October, Libra.

Venus and Mars indicate an even stronger push to earn money, with the Moon presenting some new professional opportunities. Will you take them? It's likely that at least some investigation is necessary so that you know where you stand and what your options are. You need to make your professional life and income major priorities at this time of the year.

Some of your plans may be quite big and other people may be looking at your suggestions with a degree of scepticism. This is one consequence of your actions that you need to guard against.

Being undermined by others who aren't as positive as yourself is dangerous. Avoid them, especially around the 6th.

Your inspiration is a great tonic for friends and family throughout October. With Neptune in your zone of creativity, you can help others along the path of their own creative needs. But you do need to exercise care, especially after the 16th. Outlandish, harebrained schemes that aren't practical could cause you to lose some respect among your peers. It's a good idea to draw a clear line in the sand between your professional obligations and your creative or inventive quirkiness. The two just won't mix right now.

A longstanding problem with your mother or an older female in the family may come to a head this month. Open up transparent lines of communication between the 20th and the 23rd. Certain topics may be unpalatable, uncomfortable, or could raise some eyebrows. But if you do this tastefully and don't embarrass anyone in the process, you can make some real headway and resolve differences so that your domestic environment is much more peaceful for all concerned.

You must not stop paying attention to your moods and how they affect the attitudes of your friends, particularly after the 24th. You may question or even challenge some of your friends this month. My suggestion for you is to let bygones be bygones and not to give too much attention to trivia. Personal problems are at the heart of these erratic mood swings and you shouldn't be projecting your own individual challenges onto others.

As Mars moves into your zone of short journeys on the 28th, you're ready to lash out, break free and enjoy a bit of your own personal independence. You can do this with or without a friend.

Romance and friendship

Between the 1st and the 3rd, it may be unavoidable to land yourself in some sort of dispute due to the influence of Mars and Saturn. You could be easily provoked so the onus is on you to control yourself. It's best to spend time alone and not have much to do with crowds or people in general. It's important for you to reconnect with your inner self and your spiritual values.

Adjustments to your plans will be necessary between the 6th and the 8th. Some of the appointments you make or the engagements you must attend will be more of an inconvenience than pleasurable. Try not to be negative because there's always something positive to be gained out of even the most trying of circumstances.

Negotiations between the 9th and 13th are difficult and in some ways awkward. If you've got ideas that don't sit comfortably in your social situation, you have to adapt yourself to those circumstances and see it as being for the best.

Your imagination, fantasy and creative visualisations are strong between the 15th and the 18th.

Taking up some music or art classes are excellent ways to shine your creative self to the world around you. You may also feel intuitive at this time, so trust your instincts about your personal relationships.

Intimacy and honesty can develop to an incredibly high level around the 20th. It's time to clear away the dead wood and get down to an even deeper level of maturity in the way you express yourself with your loved ones.

On the 26th, children need to be dealt with in a mature fashion. If something is not working the way you'd like it to, don't involve yourself at their level.

Work and money

It's your own indiscretion and lack of judgement in professional matters that will cause you problems between the 1st and the 3rd. Check the credentials of people before doing business with them or suffer the consequences.

During the 4th and the 8th, you must realise that achieving something often involves giving up something else. Sacrifice is the name of the game if you want big successes and, of course, the bigger the success, the greater the sacrifice.

You have to concentrate on what's important now. Don't sweat the small stuff on the 9th. On the 10th, the challenges that come your way are testing how capable you really are in what you do. This will also be a measure of your self-confidence at the end of the day.

Between the 20th and the 24th, present your ideas to people in authority. Prepare well beforehand and you'll get top marks for doing so.

You're received well between the 27th and the 30th and therefore you can expect an accolade, bonus, or possibly even a promotion in your work.

Destiny dates

Positive: 15, 17, 18, 27, 28, 29, 30

Negative: 1, 2, 3, 26

Mixed: 4, 5, 6, 7, 8, 9, 10, 11, 12, 13, 16, 20, 21, 22, 23, 24

NOVEMBER

Highlights of the month

One could argue that the three strongest forces in human nature are money, sex and power. These three superpowers may form the basis of some type of emotional manipulation that you mustn't let undermine what is otherwise a loving and nurturing relationship. Between the 3rd and the 5th, you'll note that these energies dominate the situation and could cause a rift between you and your partner or close friend. Don't let your bad moods be thecatalyst for allowing them to use emotional blackmail on you.

Between the 8th and the 12th, there'll be interesting connections with different cultures. A blending of different attitudes between yourself and another will be challenging but fun and educational. This could result in some important personal transformations for you by helping you to look at the deeper issues of your life.

A new friend on the scene, or perhaps a lover, between the 10th and the 14th is pointing you in the direction of asking some of the harder questions about your life. You could feel sensitive about opening up old wounds, but this is the only way you're going to grow and feel better about your own life, so don't fight it. Take this as a blessing in disguise.

On the 18th, both Jupiter and Venus move in direct motion, indicating clarification and a more decisive approach to work and money. You mustn't blur your vision of the people with whom you work with the actual work they have to do. Kindly ask them to produce what they need to without any bias on your part.

On the 22nd, it's a good idea to mix up your routine to bring a bit more variety and optimism to your job. Information also comes to hand regarding a new job or position within your company or profession. Expect some good news during this transit of Mars in the third zone, particularly by around the 29th, when the Sun and Venus conjoin in your zone of finances. This will be lucky for you and may even indicate an unexpected pay rise or some overlooked bonuses.

Romance and friendship

Putting your head together with people of like mind is beneficial, especially between the 7th and the 10th. This is a favourable influence for recommitting yourself to your ideals in love, and feeling that others can do the same as well will bring benefits to all concerned. This is a win–win emotional and social situation.

Take time out between the 3rd and the 5th to enjoy an outing, a drive or nature. Do nothing intense. Don't feel obligated or compelled to be running around achieving things. Humans are called 'human beings', not 'human doings'. I think you understand what I mean by this.

The doors of love open wide for you between the 11th and the 14th. A chance to meet someone new can make you feel excited and, at the same time, forgetful of your other duties or obligations. Keep a delicate balance.

Between the 16th and the 18th, if you're already committed, this could be the opportunity for you to reconnect and rediscover those original feelings that brought you and your partner together in the first place. This is an excellent period to recommit for the future.

You'll be able to communicate your feelings well between the 20th and the 24th and may even be asked to head up a social group, a party or some other function in which your communication skills will be a valuable asset.

Start that vacation on the 30th or at least get into something that gives you the chance to shut down, turn off and get creative at the same time. Recommencing that old hobby you'd pushed to the side is a good idea at this time.

Work and money

Behind the scenes work is preferred between the

1st and the 4th. You can get much done away from prying eyes and those who are too nosy for their own good. A serious tone can be expected around the 5th, even though things are going well for you financially. Perhaps you don't trust what's happening and would like to look after your future assets a little more securely. Good idea.

Confusion surrounds your investments between the 13th and the 15th. Don't take uncalculated risks and get advice before entering into areas that you're uncertain of.

You could be nervous about a meeting that you need to attend around the 17th or 18th. Be yourself. Don't pretend to be something you're not and, if you don't understand the terms or conditions, be honest enough about it to say so.

Joint finances, taxes and other banking issues will occupy your attention between the 22nd and the 24th. Once this is out of the way, your mind will be clearer, fresher, to attack new business initiatives around the 27th.

The month finishes on a good tone and some unexpected money may come your way.

Destiny dates

Positive: 1, 2, 7, 8, 9, 20, 21, 22, 23, 24, 27, 29, 30
Negative: 15, 17
Mixed: 3, 4, 10, 11, 12, 13, 14, 18, 22, 23, 24

DECEMBER

Highlights of the month

You mustn't let your concern for what people think and say about you overwhelm you. Mercury enters your domestic sphere on the 1st and gossip or news on the grapevine about family members may draw you into an endless cycle of discussion over nothing. Try to remain aloof and take everything you hear with a pinch of salt.

Projects you've commenced that have been held up will take off on the 6th, due to a more intense attitude on your part. You may have almost ditched an idea because it felt as if you were simply treading water but, by the 7th, things will be reinvigorated and you'll be ready to move full steam ahead.

The retrogression of Mercury on the 10th puts the brakes on some aspects of your communication, but you needn't let this interfere with your planning and effective execution of other areas of business. If you're working in the home as a home-maker, these transits apply equally to you, but you need to interpret this to relate to such projects around the home as gardening, refurbishing or purchasing new accessories and utensils.

The lunar eclipse on the 21st is a powerful testimony of just how spiritual your insights may be this year. At the close of 2010, you are likely to have some more aspirations triggered, which could come through a mentor or connection you least expected.

Jupiter completes 2010 in your zone of work with Uranus. Both of these planets being in retrogression indicates just a little more work is necessary to tie up loose ends before the year concludes. Your mind will feel good about your financial position and your drive and physical vitality should also be strong due to Mars's strong ambition.

Any health problems you experience in the last week of the year could benefit from being considered not just from the viewpoint of traditional medicine but also from some alternative methods. For example, investigate homeopathy, naturopathy or acupuncture. You may find greater relief by using these methods than the more common cures to which you've previously been drawn.

With Mars and the Sun strongly positing the fourth zone or family area of your horoscope after the 22nd, you'll be in the right frame of mind to entertain guests and relatives for your Christmas feast. This is an excellent conclusion to the year and, on the 30th, when Mercury goes direct, an extraordinary surprise may be the final cherry on the top of your just desserts. Enjoy, Libra!

Romance and friendship

Assert yourself between the 1st and the 4th. You have a boost of confidence and goodwill, which is attractive to others. Any projects you want to get done can be assisted by friends who will find it fun to do something different. You'll be killing two birds with one stone.

Around the 5th, take up that new regime for self-improvement. By setting an example, others will appreciate what you're doing for yourself and will follow suit.

You may have had some plans you've been looking forward to between the 6th and the 8th, but being short on cash may cause you to bail out. Destiny sometimes has other plans for us. Your duty and your desire may not mesh all that well at this time. Don't worry; there'll be other occasions to realise what you desire, so don't lose sleep over it.

Spring cleaning is necessary between the 11th and the 13th. This may have to do with your outer environments but also your inner self; your emotions and other mental attitudes. Form some new habits just now that will help you improve the quality of your relationships, both at home and in the world at large.

You need to 'seize the day'. In Latin this old saying is *Carpe Diem*! Between the 14th and the 20th, don't waste time. Make your peace with others because time waits for no one. If you've held a grudge, or others in your family have been doing the same, why not try to make peace with them? The omens are excellent and things should move forward from here on in.

Between the 22nd and the 24th, your friendships and the changes you want to effect in them may stall. Perhaps you could put this down to the Christmas rush and the fact that everyone's distracted and not all that much interested in getting down to the deep and meaningful psychological renovation that is necessary. Wait until the new year and don't push things.

Work and money

You can truly appreciate all the great things that have happened to you throughout the year and, with Jupiter passing through your zone of work, this will be accentuated. With the exception of a slightly fuzzy day on the 1st, things should improve between the 2nd and the 3rd and your planning should be very effective, indeed.

Finances are excellent around the 8th to the 10th, but try to seek a balance between your desires and what you can afford. This may be difficult with Christmas always demanding we buy bigger and better gifts for everyone else.

Do something you really, really enjoy throughout Christmas by throwing a party or, just for the heck of it, taking your friends out and shouting them to a night out on the town. You can do this to cement your friendships further, especially between the 19th and the 23rd.

After the 25th, you may need to chill out and enjoy your own company again for a while; but why not? You deserve it! It's been a big year for you and now you can sit back and enjoy the fruits of your labour. Well done, Libra.

Destiny dates

Positive: 2, 3, 4, 5, 9, 11, 12, 13, 14, 15, 16, 17, 18, 19, 20, 21, 25, 30

Negative: nil

Mixed: 1, 6, 7, 8, 10, 22, 23, 24

2010:
Astronumerology

Never allow someone to be your priority while allowing yourself to be their option.

—Anonymous

The power behind your name

By adding the numbers of your name you can see which planet is ruling you. Each of the letters of the alphabet is assigned a number, which is listed below. These numbers are ruled by the planets. This is according to the ancient Chaldean system of numerology and is very different to the Pythagorean system to which many refer.

Each number is assigned a planet:

AIQJY	=	1	**Sun**
BKR	=	2	**Moon**
CGLS	=	3	**Jupiter**
DMT	=	4	**Uranus**
EHNX	=	5	**Mercury**
UVW	=	6	**Venus**
OZ	=	7	**Neptune**
FP	=	8	**Saturn**
—	=	9	**Mars**

Notice that the number 9 is not aligned with a letter because it is considered special. Once the numbers have been added you will see that a single planet rules your name and personal affairs. Many famous actors, writers and musicians change their names to attract the energy of a luckier planet. You can experiment with the list and try new names or add the letters of your second name to see how that vibration suits you. It's a lot of fun!

Here is an example of how to find out the power of your name. If your name is John Smith, calculate the ruling planet by assigning each letter to a number in the table like this:

J O H N S M I T H
1 7 5 5   3 4 1 4 5

Now add the numbers like this:
1 + 7 + 5 + 5 + 3 + 4 + 1 + 4 + 5 = 35
Then add 3 + 5 = 8

The ruling number of John Smith's name is 8, which is ruled by Saturn. Now study the name-number table to reveal the power of your name. The numbers 3 and 5 will also play a secondary role in John's character and destiny, so in this case you would also study the effects of Jupiter and Mercury.

Name-number table

Your name number	Ruling planet	Your name characteristics
1	**Sun**	Magnetic individual. Great energy and life force. Physically dynamic and sociable. Attracts good friends and individuals in powerful positions. Good government connections. Intelligent, impressive, flashy and victorious. A loyal number for relationships.
2	**Moon**	Soft, emotional nature. Changeable moods but psychic, intuitive senses. Imaginative nature and empathetic expression of feelings. Loves family, mother and home life. Night owl who probably needs more sleep. Success with the public and/or women.
3	**Jupiter**	Outgoing, optimistic number with lucky overtones. Attracts opportunities without trying. Good sense of timing. Religious or spiritual aspirations.

Your name number	Ruling planet	Your name characteristics
		Can investigate the meaning of life. Loves to travel and explore the world and people.
4	Uranus	Explosive character with many unusual aspects. Likes the untried and novel. Forward thinking, with many extraordinary friends. Gets fed up easily so needs plenty of invigorating experiences. Pioneering, technological and imaginative. Wilful and stubborn when wants to be. Unexpected events in life may be positive or negative.
5	Mercury	Quick-thinking mind with great powers of speech. Extremely vigorous life; always on the go and lives on nervous energy. Youthful attitude and never grows old. Looks younger than actual age. Young friends and humorous disposition. Loves reading and writing.
6	Venus	Delightful personality. Graceful and attractive character who cherishes friends

148

Your name number	Ruling planet	Your name characteristics
		and social life. Musical or artistic interests. Good for money making as well as abundant love affairs. Career in the public eye is possible. Loves family but is often overly concerned by friends.
7	Neptune	Intuitive, spiritual and self-sacrificing nature. Easily misled by those who need help. Loves to dream of life's possibilities. Has curative powers. Dreams are revealing and prophetic. Loves the water and will have many journeys in life. Spiritual aspirations dominate worldly desires.
8	Saturn	Hard-working, focused individual with slow but certain success. Incredible concentration and self-sacrifice for a goal.
		Money orientated but generous when trust is gained. Professional but may be a hard taskmaster. Demands

highest standards and needs to learn to enjoy life a little more.

9	**Mars**	Fantastic physical drive and ambition. Sports and outdoor activities are keys to wellbeing. Confrontational. Likes to work and play just as hard. Caring and protective of family, friends and territory. Individual tastes in life but is also self-absorbed. Needs to listen to others' advice to gain greater success.

Your 2010 planetary ruler

Astrology and numerology are very intimately connected. As already shown, each planet rules over a number between 1 and 9. Both your name *and* your birth date are ruled by planetary energies.

Add the numbers of your birth date and the year in question to find out which planet will control the coming year for you.

For example, if you were born on the 12th of November, add the numerals 1 and 2 (12, your day of birth) and 1 and 1 (11, your month of birth) to the year in question, in this case 2010 (the current year), like this:

$$1 + 2 + 1 + 1 + 2 + 0 + 1 + 0 = 8$$

The planet ruling your individual karma for 2010 will be Saturn because this planet rules the number 8.

You can even take your ruling name-number as shown earlier and add it to the year in question to throw more light on your coming personal affairs, like this:

John Smith = 8

Year coming = 2010

$8 + 2 + 0 + 1 + 0 = 11$

$1 + 1 = 2$

Therefore, 2 is the ruling number of the combined name and date vibrations. Study the Moon's number 2 influence for 2010.

Outlines of the year number ruled by each planet are given below. Enjoy!

1 is the year of the Sun

Overview

The Sun is the brightest object in the heavens and rules number 1 and the sign of Leo. Because of this the coming year will bring you great success and popularity.

You'll be full of life and radiant vibrations and are more than ready to tackle your new nine-year cycle, which begins now. Any new projects you commence are likely to be successful.

Your health and vitality will be very strong and your stamina at its peak. Even if you happen to have the odd problem with your health, your recuperative power will be strong.

You have tremendous magnetism this year so social popularity won't be a problem for you. I see many new friends and lovers coming into your life. Expect loads of invitations to parties and fun-filled outings. Just don't take your health for granted as you're likely to burn the candle at both ends.

With success coming your way, don't let it go to your head. You must maintain humility, which will make you even more popular in the coming year.

Love and pleasure

This is an important cycle for renewing your love and connections with your family, particularly if you have children. The Sun is connected with the sign of Leo and therefore brings an increase in musical and theatrical activities. Entertainment and other creative hobbies will be high on your agenda and bring you a great sense of satisfaction.

Work

You won't have to make too much of an effort to be successful this year because the brightness of the Sun will draw opportunities to you. Changes in work are likely and, if you have been concerned that opportunities are few and far between, 2010 will be different. You can expect some sort of promotion or an increase in income because your employers will take special note of your skills and service orientation.

Improving your luck

Leo is the ruler of number 1 and, therefore, if you're born under this star sign, 2010 will be particularly lucky. For others, July and August, the months of Leo, will bring good fortune. The 1st, 8th, 15th and 22nd hours of Sundays especially will give you a unique sort of luck in any sort of competition or activities generally. Keep your eye out for those born under Leo as they may be able to contribute something to your life and may even have a karmic connection to you. This is a particularly important year for your destiny.

Your lucky numbers in this coming cycle are 1, 10, 19 and 28.

2 is the year of the Moon

Overview

There's nothing more soothing than the cool light of the full Moon on a clear night. The Moon is emotional and receptive and controls your destiny in 2010. If you're able to use the positive energies of the Moon, it will be a great year in which you can realign and improve your relationships, particularly with family members.

Making a commitment to becoming a better person and bringing your emotions under control will also dominate your thinking. Try not to let your emotions get the better of you throughout the coming year because you may be drawn into the changeable nature of these lunar vibrations as well. If you fail to keep control of your emotional life you'll later regret some of your actions. You must blend careful thinking with feeling to arrive at the best results. Your luck throughout 2010 will certainly be determined by the state of your mind.

Because the Moon and the sign of Cancer rule the number 2 there is a certain amount of change to be expected this year. Keep your feelings steady and don't let your heart rule your head.

Love and pleasure

Your primary concern in 2010 will be your home and family life. You'll be finally keen to take on those renovations, or work on your garden. You may even think of buying a new home. You can at last carry out some of those plans and make your dreams come true. If you find yourself a little more temperamental than usual, do some extra meditation and spend time alone until you sort this out. You mustn't withhold your feelings from your partner as this will only create frustration.

Work

During 2010 your focus will be primarily on feelings and family; however, this doesn't mean you can't make great strides in your work as well. The Moon rules the general public and what you might find is that special opportunities and connections with the world at large present themselves to you. You could be working with large numbers of people.

If you're looking for a better work opportunity, try to focus your attention on women who can give you a hand. Use your intuition as it will be finely tuned this year. Work and career success depends upon your instincts.

Improving your luck

The sign of Cancer is your ruler this year and because the Moon rules Mondays, both this day of the week and the month of July are extremely lucky for you. The 1st, 8th, 15th and 22nd hours on Mondays will be very powerful. Pay special attention to the new and full Moon days throughout 2010.

The numbers 2, 11 and 29 are lucky for you.

3 is the year of Jupiter

Overview

The year 2010 will be a number 3 year for you and, because of this, Jupiter and Sagittarius will dominate your affairs. This is extremely lucky and shows you'll be motivated to broaden your horizons, gain more money and become extremely popular in your social circles. It looks like 2010 will be a fun-filled year with much excitement.

Jupiter and Sagittarius are generous to a fault and so, likewise, your open-handedness will mark the year. You'll be friendly and helpful to all of those around you.

Pisces is also under the rulership of the number 3 and this brings out your spiritual and compassionate nature. You'll become a much better person, reducing your negative karma by increasing your self-awareness and spiritual feelings. You will want to share your luck with those you love.

Love and pleasure

Travel and seeking new adventures will be part and parcel of your romantic life this year. Travelling to distant lands and meeting unusual people will open your heart to fresh possibilities of romance.

You'll try novel and audacious things and will find yourself in a different circle of friends. Compromise will be important in making your existing relationships work. Talk about your feelings. If you are currently in a relationship you'll feel an upswing in your affection for your partner. This is a perfect opportunity to deepen your love for each other and take your relationship to a new level.

If you're not yet attached to someone, there's good news for you. Great opportunities lie in store and a spiritual or karmic connection may be experienced in 2010.

Work

Great fortune can be expected through your working life in the next twelve months. Your friends and work colleagues will want to help you achieve your goals. Even your employers will be amenable to your requests for extra money or a better position within the organisation.

If you want to start a new job or possibly begin an independent line of business, this is a great year to do it. Jupiter looks set to give you plenty of opportunities, success and a superior reputation.

Improving your luck

As long as you can keep a balanced view of things and not overdo anything, your luck will increase dramatically throughout 2010. The important thing is to remain grounded and not be too airy-fairy about your objectives. Be realistic about your talents and capabilities and don't brag about your skills or achievements. This will only invite envy from others.

Moderate your social life as well and don't drink or eat too much as this will slow your reflexes and weaken your chances for success.

You have plenty of spiritual insights this year so you should use them to their maximum. In the 1st, 8th, 15th and 24th hours of Thursdays you should use your intuition to enhance your luck, and the numbers 3, 12, 21 and 30 are also lucky for you. March and December are your lucky months but generally the whole year should go pretty smoothly for you.

4 is the year of Uranus

Overview

The electric and exciting planet of the zodiac, Uranus, and its sign of Aquarius, rule your affairs throughout 2010. Dramatic events will surprise and at the same time unnerve you in your professional and personal life. So be prepared!

You'll be able to achieve many things this year and your dreams are likely to come true, but you mustn't be distracted or scattered with your energies. You'll be breaking through your own self-limitations and this will present challenges from your family and friends. You'll want to be independent and develop your spiritual powers and nothing will stop you.

Try to maintain discipline and an orderly lifestyle so you can make the most of these special energies this year. If unexpected things do happen, it's not a bad idea to have an alternative plan so you don't lose momentum.

Love and pleasure

You want something radical, something different in your relationships this year. It's quite likely that your love life will be feeling a little less than exciting so you'll take some important steps to change that. If your partner is as progressive as you'll be this year, then your relationship is likely to improve and fulfil both of you.

In your social life you will meet some very unusual people, whom you'll feel are especially connected to you spiritually. You may want to ditch everything for the excitement and passion of a completely new relationship, but tread carefully as this may not work out exactly as you expect it to.

Work

Technology, computing and the Internet will play a larger role in your professional life this coming year.

You'll have to move ahead with the times and learn new skills if you want to achieve success.

A hectic schedule is likely, so make sure your diary is with you at all times. Try to be more efficient and don't waste time.

New friends and alliances at work will help you achieve even greater success in the coming period. Becoming a team player will be even more important in gaining satisfaction from your professional endeavours.

Improving your luck

Moving too quickly and impulsively will cause you problems on all fronts, so be a little more patient and think your decisions through more carefully. Social, romantic and professional opportunities will come to you but take a little time to investigate the ramifications of your actions.

The 1st, 8th, 15th and 20th hours of any Saturday are lucky, but love and luck are likely to cross your path when you least expect it. The numbers 4, 13, 22 and 31 are also lucky for you this year.

5 is the year of Mercury

Overview

The supreme planet of communication, Mercury, is your ruling planet throughout 2010. The number 5, which is connected to Mercury, will confer upon you success through your intellectual abilities.

Any form of writing or speaking will be improved and this will be, to a large extent, underpinning your success. Your imagination will be stimulated by this planet, with many incredible new and exciting ideas coming to mind.

Mercury and the number 5 are considered somewhat indecisive. Be firm in your attitude and don't let too many ideas or opportunities distract and confuse you. By all means get as much information as you can to help you make the right decisions.

I see you involved with money proposals, job applications, even contracts that need to be signed, so remain as clear-headed as possible.

Your business skills and clear and concise communication will be at the heart of your life in 2010.

Love and pleasure

Mercury, which rules the signs of Gemini and Virgo, will make your love life a little difficult due to its changeable nature. On the one hand you'll feel passionate and loving to your partner, yet on the other you will feel like giving it all up for the excitement of a new affair. Maintain the middle ground.

Also, try not to be too critical with your friends and family members. The influence of Virgo makes you prone to expecting much more from others than they're capable of giving. Control your sharp tongue and don't hurt people's feelings. Encouraging others is the better path, leading to greater emotional satisfaction.

Work

Speed will dominate your professional life in 2010. You'll be flitting from one subject to another and taking on far more than you can handle. You'll need to make some serious changes in your routine to handle the avalanche of work that will come your way. You'll also be travelling with your work, but not necessarily overseas.

If you're in a job you enjoy then this year will give you additional successes. If not, it may be time to move on.

Improving your luck

Communication is the key to attaining your desires in the coming twelve months. Keep focused on one idea rather than scattering your energies in all directions and your success will be speedier.

By looking after your health, sleeping well and exercising regularly, you'll build up your resilience and mental strength.

The 1st, 8th, 15th and 20th hours of Wednesday are lucky so it's best to schedule your meetings and other important social engagements during these times. The lucky numbers for Mercury are 5, 14, 23 and 32.

6 is the year of Venus

Overview

Because you're ruled by 6 this year, love is in the air! Venus, Taurus and Libra are well known for their affinity with romance, love, and even marriage. If ever you were going to meet a soulmate and feel comfortable in love, 2010 must surely be your year.

Taurus has a strong connection to money and practical affairs as well, so finances will also improve if you are diligent about work and security issues.

The important thing to keep in mind this year is that sharing love and making that important soul connection should be kept high on your agenda. This will be an enjoyable period in your life.

Love and pleasure

Romance is the key thing for you this year and your current relationships will become more fulfilling if you happen to be attached. For singles, a 6 year heralds an important meeting that eventually leads to marriage.

You'll also be interested in fashion, gifts, jewellery and all sorts of socialising. It's at one of these social engagements that you could meet the love of your life. Remain available!

Venus is one of the planets that has a tendency to overdo things, so be moderate in your eating and drinking. Try generally to maintain a modest lifestyle.

Work

You'll have a clearer insight into finances and your future security during a number 6 year. Whereas previously you may have had additional expenses and extra distractions, your mind will now be more settled and capable of longer-term planning along these lines.

With the extra cash you might see this year, decorating your home or office will give you a special sort of satisfaction.

Social affairs and professional activities will be strongly linked. Any sort of work-related functions may offer you romantic opportunities as well. On the other hand, be careful not to mix up your workplace relationships with romantic ideals. This could complicate some of your professional activities.

Improving your luck

You'll want more money and a life of leisure and ease in 2010. Keep working on your strengths and eliminate your negative personality traits to create greater luck and harmony in your life.

Moderate all your actions and don't focus exclusively on money and material objects. Feed your spiritual needs as well. By balancing your inner and outer sides you'll see that your romantic and professional lives will be enhanced more easily.

The 1st, 8th, 15th and 20th hours on Fridays will be very lucky for you and new opportunities will arise for you at those times. You can use the numbers 6, 15, 24 and 33 to increase luck in your general affairs.

7 is the year of Neptune

Overview

The last and most evolved sign of the zodiac is

Pisces, which is ruled by Neptune. The number 7 is deeply connected with this zodiac sign and governs you in 2010. Your ideals seem to be clearer and more spiritually orientated than ever before. Your desire to evolve and understand your inner self will be a double-edged sword. It depends on how organised you are as to how well you can use these spiritual and abstract concepts in your practical life.

Your past hurts and deep emotional issues will be dealt with and removed for good, if you are serious about becoming a better human being.

Spend a little more time caring for yourself rather than others, as it's likely some of your friends will drain you of energy with their own personal problems. Of course, you mustn't turn a blind eye to the needs of others, but don't ignore your own personal requirements in the process.

Love and pleasure

Meeting people with similar life views and spiritual aspirations will rekindle your faith in relationships. If you do choose to develop a new romance, make sure there is a clear understanding of the responsibilities of one to the other. Don't get swept off your feet by people who have ulterior motives.

Keep your relationships realistic and see that the most idealistic partnerships must eventually come down to Earth. Deal with the practicalities of life.

Work

This is a year of hard work, but one in which you'll

come to understand the deeper significance of your professional ideals. You may discover a whole new aspect to your career, which involves a more compassionate and self-sacrificing side to your personality.

You'll also find that your way of working will change and you'll be more focused and able to get into the spirit of whatever you do. Finding meaningful work is very likely and therefore this could be a year when money, security, creativity and spirituality overlap to bring you a great sense of personal satisfaction.

Tapping into your greater self through meditation and self-study will bring you great benefits throughout 2010.

Improving your luck

Using self-sacrifice along with discrimination will be an unusual method of improving your luck. The laws of karma state that what you give, you receive in greater measure. This is one of the principal themes for you in 2010.

The 1st, 8th, 15th and 20th hours of Tuesdays are your lucky times. The numbers 7, 16, 25 and 34 should be used to increase your lucky energies.

8 is the year of Saturn

Overview

The earthy and practical sign of Capricorn and its ruler Saturn are intimately linked to the number 8, which rules you in 2010. Your discipline and far-sightedness will help you achieve great things in the coming year. With cautious discernment, slowly but surely you will reach your goals.

It may be that due to the influence of the solitary Saturn, your best work and achievement will be behind closed doors away from the limelight. You mustn't fear this as you'll discover many new things about yourself. You'll learn just how strong you really are.

Love and pleasure

Work will overshadow your personal affairs in 2010, but you mustn't let this erode the personal relationships you have. Becoming a workaholic brings great material successes but will also cause you to become too insular and aloof. Your family members won't take too kindly to you working 100-hour weeks.

Responsibility is one of the key words for this number and you will therefore find yourself in a position of authority that leaves very little time for fun. Try to make the time to enjoy the company of friends and family and by all means schedule time off on the weekends as it will give you the peace of mind you're looking for.

Because of your responsible attitude it will be very hard for you not to assume a greater role in your workplace and this indicates longer working hours with the likelihood of a promotion with equally good remuneration.

Work

Money is high on your agenda in 2010. Number 8 is a good money number according to the Chinese and this year is at last likely to bring you the fruits of your hard labour. You are cautious and resourceful in all your dealings and will not waste your hard-earned savings. You will also be very conscious of using your time wisely.

You will be given more responsibilities and you're likely to take them on, if only to prove to yourself that you can handle whatever life dishes up.

Expect a promotion in which you'll play a leading role in your work. Your diligence and hard work will pay off, literally, in a bigger salary and more respect from others.

Improving your luck

Caution is one of the key characteristics of the number 8 and is linked to Capricorn. But being overly cautious could cause you to miss valuable opportunities. If an offer is put to you, try to think outside the square and balance it with your naturally cautious nature.

Be gentle and kind to yourself. By loving yourself, others will naturally love you, too. The 1st, 8th, 15th and 20th hours of Saturdays are exceptionally lucky for you, as are the numbers 1, 8, 17, 26 and 35.

9 is the year of Mars

Overview

You are now entering the final year of a nine-year cycle dominated by the planet Mars and the sign of Aries. You'll be completing many things and are determined to be successful after several years of intense work.

Some of your relationships may now have reached their use-by date and even personal affairs may need to be released. Don't let arguments and disagreements get in the road of friendly resolution in these areas of your life.

Mars is a challenging planet, and this year, although you will be very active and productive, you may find others trying to obstruct the achievement of your goals. As a result you may react strongly to them, thereby creating disharmony in your workplace. Don't be so impulsive or reckless, and generally slow things down. The slower, steadier approach has greater merit this year.

Love and pleasure

If you become too bossy and pushy with friends this year you will just end up pushing them out of your life. It's a year to end certain friendships but by the same token it could be the perfect time to remove conflicts and thereby bolster your love affairs in 2010.

If you're feeling a little irritable and angry with those you love, try getting rid of these negative feelings through some intense, rigorous sports and physical activity. This will definitely relieve tension and improve your personal life.

Work

Because you're healthy and able to work at a more intense pace you'll achieve an incredible amount in the coming year. Overwork could become a problem if you're not careful.

Because the number 9 and Mars are infused with leadership energy, you'll be asked to take the reins of the job and steer your company or group in a certain direction. This will bring with it added responsibility but also a greater sense of purpose for you.

Improving your luck

Because of the hot and restless energy of the number 9, it is important to create more mental peace in your life this year. Lower the temperature, so to speak, and decompress your relationships rather than becoming aggravated. Try to talk with your work partners and loved ones rather than telling them what to do. This will generally pick up your health and your relationships.

The 1st, 8th, 15th and 20th hours of Tuesdays are the luckiest for you this year and, if you're involved in any disputes or need to attend to health issues, these times are also very good to get the best results. Your lucky numbers are 9, 18, 27 and 36.

2010:
Your Daily Planner

*If you only do what you know you can do, you will
never do very much.*

—Tom Krause

According to astrology, the success of any venture or
activity is dependent upon the planetary positions
at the time you commence that activity. Electional
astrology helps you select the most appropriate
times for many of your day-to-day endeavours.
These dates are applicable to each and every zodiac
sign and can be used freely by one and all, even if
your star sign doesn't fall under the one mentioned
in this book. Please note that the daily planner is a
universal system applicable equally to all *twelve* star
signs. Anyone and everyone can use this planner
irrespective of their birth sign.

Ancient astrologers understood the planetary
patterns and how they impacted on each of us. This
allowed them to suggest the best possible times
to start various important activities. For example,
many farmers still use this approach today: they
understand the phases of the Moon, and attest to
the fact that planting seeds on certain lunar days
produces a far better crop than does planting on
other days.

In the following section, many facets of daily
life are considered. Using the lunar cycle and the
combined strength of other planets allows us to
work out the best times to do them. This is your
personal almanac, which can be used in conjunction with any star sign to help optimise the results.

First, select the activity you are interested in, and then quickly scan the year for the best months to start it. When you have selected the month, you can finetune your timing by finding the best specific dates. You can then be sure that the planetary energies will be in sync with you, offering you the best possible outcome.

Coupled with what you know about your monthly and weekly trends, the daily planner is an effective tool to help you capitalise on opportunities that come your way this year.

Good luck, and may the planets bless you with great success, fortune and happiness in 2010!

Getting started in 2010

How many times have you made a new year's resolution to begin a diet or be a better person in your relationships? And, how many times has it not worked out? Well, part of the reason may be that you started out at the wrong time, because how successful you are is strongly influenced by the position of the Moon and the planets when you begin a particular activity. You will be more successful with the following endeavours if you start them on the days indicated.

Relationships

We all feel more empowered on some days than on others. This is because the planets have some power over us—their movement and their relationships to each other determine the ebb and flow of our energies. And, our levels of self-confidence and sense of romantic magnetism play an important part in the way we behave in relationships.

Your daily planner tells you the ideal dates for meeting new friends, initiating a love affair, spending time with family and loved ones—it even tells you the most appropriate times for sexual encounters.

You'll be surprised at how much more impact you will make in your relationships when you tune yourself in to the planetary energies on these special dates.

Falling in love/restoring love

During these times you could expect favourable energies to meet your soulmate or, if you've had difficulty in a relationship, to approach the one you love to rekindle both your and their emotional responses:

January	18, 20, 23, 24
February	15, 16, 20, 24
March	29
April	16
May	14, 17, 18, 19, 20, 23
June	14, 15, 16, 20, 21
July	12
August	10, 13, 14
September	9, 21, 22
October	8, 18, 19, 20
November	14, 15, 16, 19, 20, 21
December	13, 17, 18

Special times with friends and family

Socialising, partying and having a good time with those whose company you enjoy is highly favourable under the following dates. They are excellent to spend time with family and loved ones in a domestic environment:

January	6, 26, 27
February	12, 13, 14, 15, 16, 20, 24
March	11, 21, 22, 29, 30, 31
April	8
May	15, 16, 17, 18, 19, 20, 23, 24
June	1, 2, 3, 11, 12, 14, 15, 16, 20, 21, 29, 30
July	8, 9, 12, 17, 18, 26, 27
August	5, 6, 9, 10, 13, 14, 22, 23, 24
September	1, 2, 5, 9, 10, 18, 19, 20, 30
October	3, 19, 20, 25, 26, 30, 31
November	3, 4, 14, 15, 16, 22, 26, 27
December	2, 9, 10, 11, 19, 20, 24, 25

Healing or resuming relationships

If you're trying to get back together with the one you love or need a heart-to-heart or deep-and-meaningful discussion with someone, you can try the following dates to do so:

January	12, 13, 14, 15, 21, 22, 23, 24, 25
February	6
March	6, 31
April	2, 7, 8, 12, 16, 19, 23, 24, 25, 26

May	10, 11, 12, 13, 14, 15, 16, 17, 18, 19, 20, 21, 22, 23, 24, 25, 26, 27, 28, 30
June	3, 8, 9, 10, 11, 12, 13, 14, 15, 16, 17, 21, 22, 23, 25, 26, 27, 28, 29, 30
July	1, 2, 3, 4, 5, 10, 11, 12, 13, 15, 16, 17, 18, 19, 20, 21, 22, 23, 28, 29, 30
August	1, 2, 3, 4, 5, 6, 9, 10, 13, 14, 15, 16, 20, 23, 25, 26, 27
September	2, 5, 9, 10, 13, 17, 18, 19, 20
October	1, 2, 3, 6, 12, 13, 14, 15, 20, 22, 23, 24, 25, 26, 27, 28, 29, 30, 31
November	3, 4, 5, 6, 7, 8, 9, 21, 27, 28, 29, 30
December	2, 3, 4, 6, 12, 13, 14, 17, 18, 19, 20, 21, 23, 24, 25

Sexual encounters

Physical and sexual energies are well favoured on the following dates. The energies of the planets enhance your moments of intimacy during these times:

January	1, 6, 7, 21, 22
February	6, 12, 13, 14, 20, 24
March	14, 15, 17, 18, 19, 30, 31
April	23, 24, 25, 26
May	9, 12, 14, 17, 18, 19, 20
June	3, 8, 9, 10, 11, 14, 15, 16, 20, 21, 29, 30
July	8, 9, 10, 11, 12
August	6, 10, 13, 14, 22, 23, 24

September   3, 4, 5, 6, 9, 10, 18, 19, 20, 21, 22, 30

October   1, 2, 3, 7, 8, 18, 19, 20, 23, 24, 28, 29, 30, 31

November   3, 4, 14, 15, 16, 19, 24, 25, 26, 27

December   2, 10, 11, 12, 13, 15, 16, 17, 19, 20, 22, 23, 24, 25

Health and wellbeing

Your aura and life force are susceptible to the movements of the planets—in particular, they respond to the phases of the Moon.

The following dates are the most appropriate times to begin a diet, have cosmetic surgery, or seek medical advice. They also indicate the best times to help others.

Feeling of wellbeing

Your physical as well as your mental alertness should be strong on these following dates. You can plan your activities and expect a good response from others:

January   2, 3, 4, 5, 6, 7, 11, 12, 13, 14, 16, 17, 18, 21, 22, 23, 24, 30, 31

February   1, 2, 7, 8, 15, 16, 17, 18, 19, 20, 21, 22, 23, 24, 25, 26, 27, 28

March   16, 17, 18, 19, 20, 22, 23, 24, 25, 26, 27, 28, 29

April   7, 13, 14, 16, 28

May   2, 11, 14, 25, 26

June   8, 22, 23, 26, 27, 28, 29, 30

July	4, 5, 8, 9, 12, 13, 14, 15, 16, 19, 20, 23, 24, 25
August	5, 6, 9, 10, 11, 12, 13, 15, 16, 20, 21
September	9, 10, 11, 12, 13, 16, 17, 21, 22, 24, 25, 28, 29, 30
October	3, 4, 5, 6, 7, 8, 9, 10, 13, 14, 15, 22
November	4, 5, 6, 10, 11, 19, 20, 21
December	7, 8, 17, 18, 28, 29

Healing and medicine

These times are good for approaching others who have expertise when you need some deeper understanding. They are also favourable for any sort of healing or medication and making appointments with doctors or psychologists. Planning surgery around these dates should bring good results.

Often giving up our time and energy to assist others doesn't necessarily result in the expected outcome. However, by lending a helping hand to a friend on the following dates, the results should be favourable:

January	1, 2, 3, 4, 6, 7, 8, 9, 11, 12, 13, 14, 15, 16, 17, 18, 19, 20, 21, 22, 23, 24, 26, 27, 28, 29, 30, 31
February	1, 5, 6, 9, 11, 12, 13, 14, 15, 16, 19
March	1, 2, 3, 4, 5, 8, 9, 10, 11, 12, 18, 19, 24, 25, 29
April	1, 3, 4, 5, 22, 26
May	4, 5

June	1, 2, 3, 9, 10, 17, 18, 22, 23, 24, 25, 29, 30
July	6, 7, 15, 16, 17, 18, 19, 21, 22, 23, 24, 25, 26
August	2, 3, 4, 11, 12, 17, 18, 19, 20, 21, 30, 31
September	6, 7, 8, 10, 11, 12, 13, 14, 15, 16, 17, 18, 26, 27, 28, 29
October	5, 7, 8, 9, 10, 11, 12, 13, 14, 15, 16, 17, 18, 19, 20, 21, 22, 23, 24, 25, 26, 28, 29, 30, 31
November	1, 2, 3, 5, 7, 8, 10, 11, 14, 15, 17, 18, 19, 22, 23
December	4, 5, 7, 8, 9, 10, 12, 13, 14, 16, 23, 24, 25, 26, 28, 29, 30, 31

Money

Money is an important part of life, and involves many decisions—decisions about borrowing, investing, spending. The ideal times for transactions are very much influenced by the planets, and whether your investment or nest egg grows or doesn't grow can often be linked to timing. Making your decisions on the following dates could give you a whole new perspective on your financial future.

Managing wealth and money

To build your nest egg it's a good time to open your bank account or invest money on the following dates:

January	1, 6, 7, 13, 14, 15, 18, 21, 22, 28, 29
February	3, 4, 9, 10, 11, 12, 13, 14, 15, 17, 18, 24, 25

March	2, 3, 9, 10, 16, 17, 18, 23, 24, 29, 30, 31
April	5, 6, 7, 13, 14, 19, 20, 21, 26, 27,
May	2, 3, 4, 10, 11, 17, 18, 23, 24, 30, 31
June	6, 7, 8, 13, 14, 19, 20, 21, 26, 27, 28
July	4, 5, 10, 11, 12, 17, 18, 23, 24, 25, 31
August	1, 7, 8, 13, 14, 20, 21, 27, 28, 29
September	3, 4, 9, 10, 16, 17, 23, 24, 25
October	1, 2, 7, 8, 13, 14, 15, 21, 22, 28, 29
November	3, 4, 10, 11, 17, 18, 24, 25
December	1, 2, 7, 8, 14, 15, 16, 21, 22, 23, 24, 29

Spending

It's always fun to spend but the following dates are more in tune with this activity and are likely to give you better results:

January	3, 4, 5, 6, 7, 8, 9, 10, 11, 12, 13, 14
February	3, 4, 5, 10, 19
March	8, 10, 11, 13, 14, 19
April	7, 8, 11, 12, 22
May	6, 7, 8, 9, 10, 11, 12, 13, 17, 18, 19, 20, 21, 22, 23, 24, 25, 26, 27, 28
June	1, 11, 12, 14, 16, 17, 19, 23, 25, 26, 27, 28, 29, 30
July	6, 7, 8, 23, 24, 25, 26, 27, 28, 29, 31
August	1, 2, 3, 4, 5, 15, 16, 17, 18, 19, 30, 31
September	1, 2, 3, 4, 17, 18, 19, 20, 21, 22, 23, 27, 28, 29, 30

October	4, 7, 12, 13, 14, 15, 16, 17, 18, 19, 27, 28
November	2, 3, 4, 25, 26, 27, 28
December	11, 22, 23

Selling

If you're thinking of selling something, whether it is small or large, consider the following dates as ideal times to do so:

January	18
February	12, 13, 14, 15
March	5, 6, 9, 14, 15, 16, 17, 18, 19, 21
April	1, 3, 4, 5, 22, 26
May	7, 12, 21, 29
June	3, 8, 9, 10, 11, 12, 13, 17, 24, 25, 26, 27, 28, 30
July	1, 2, 7, 9, 10, 11, 25, 27, 28, 29, 30, 31
August	1, 2, 3, 4, 5, 6, 7, 8, 9, 10, 13, 20, 23, 28
September	2, 9, 10, 11, 12, 13, 14, 15, 16, 17, 18, 19, 20, 21, 22, 23, 24, 26, 30
October	1, 2, 3, 4, 6, 7, 10, 11, 17, 18, 19, 20, 21, 22, 23, 24, 25, 27, 29
November	3, 4, 5, 6, 7, 11, 14, 15, 16, 17, 18, 19, 21, 23, 24, 25, 26, 27, 28, 29, 30
December	1, 2, 3, 4, 5, 6, 7, 8, 9, 10, 11, 12, 13, 14, 15, 16, 17, 18, 19, 20, 21, 22

Borrowing

Few of us like to borrow money, but if you must, taking out a loan on the following dates will be positive:

January	12, 30
February	7, 12, 13
March	6, 7, 8, 11
April	3, 4, 8
May	9, 28, 29
June	1, 2, 3, 4, 5, 29, 30
July	1, 2, 3, 26, 27, 28, 29, 30
August	9, 25, 26
September	5, 6
October	3, 30
November	26, 27
December	3, 4, 21, 22, 23, 30, 31

Work and education

Your career is important, and continual improvement of your skills is therefore also crucial professionally, mentally and socially. The dates below will help you find out the most appropriate times to improve your professional talents and commence new work or education associated with your work.

You may need to decide when to start learning a new skill, when to ask for a promotion, and even when to make an important career change. Here are the days when your mental and educational power is strong.

Learning new skills

Educational pursuits are lucky and bring good results on the following dates:

January	15, 16, 17, 18, 19, 20, 21, 22, 25, 26, 27
February	14, 15, 16, 17, 18, 19, 22, 23, 28
March	16, 17, 18, 21, 22, 27, 28
April	17, 18, 24, 25
May	15, 16, 21, 22
June	12, 17, 18, 24, 25
July	15, 16, 21, 22, 23, 24, 25
August	11, 12, 17, 18, 19
September	8, 13, 15, 20, 21, 22
October	11, 12
November	7, 8, 9
December	6, 19, 20

Changing career path or profession

If you're feeling stuck and need to move into a new professional activity, changing jobs could be done at these times:

January	6, 7, 15, 16, 17, 23, 24
February	12, 13, 14, 19, 20, 21
March	19, 20, 27, 28
April	15, 16, 24, 25
May	14, 21, 22
June	17, 18, 19, 20, 21
July	8, 9, 15, 16, 23, 24, 25

August	5, 6, 11, 12, 20, 21, 22, 23
September	1, 2, 8, 13, 14, 15, 17
October	8, 13, 14, 15, 16, 17
November	3, 4, 10, 11, 19, 20, 21
December	1, 2, 3, 7, 8, 17, 18, 28, 29

Promotion, professional focus and hard work

To increase your mental focus and achieve good results from the work you do; promotions are also likely on these dates:

January	4, 5, 6, 11, 12, 13, 14, 15, 16, 17, 18, 19, 21
February	6
March	16, 17, 18, 19, 20, 21, 23, 24, 25, 26, 27, 28, 29
April	8, 28, 29
May	12, 21
June	25, 26, 27, 28
July	4, 5, 8, 9, 12, 13, 14, 15, 16, 17, 18, 19, 20, 21, 22, 23, 24, 25, 26, 27
August	5, 6, 10, 11, 12, 13, 14, 15, 16, 17, 18, 19, 20, 21, 22, 23, 24
September	13, 14, 15
October	10, 11, 12, 13, 14, 15, 17, 18, 19, 20, 22, 23, 24, 30, 31
November	2, 4, 5, 6, 7, 8, 9, 23, 24, 25, 26, 27, 28, 29, 30
December	2, 3, 4, 11, 12, 13, 14, 15, 16, 18, 19, 20, 21, 23, 24, 25

Travel

Setting out on a holiday or adventurous journey is exciting. Here are the most favourable times for doing this. Travel on the following dates is likely to give you a sense of fulfilment:

January	15
February	15, 16, 18, 19, 20, 21
March	16, 17, 18, 21, 22, 23
April	19, 24, 25, 26, 27
May	16, 17, 18, 21, 22
June	17, 18, 19, 20, 21, 24, 25
July	21, 22, 23, 24, 25
August	19
September	9, 21, 22
October	18, 19, 20, 21, 22
November	7, 16, 17, 18
December	6, 14, 16, 19, 20

Beauty and grooming

Believe it or not, cutting your hair or nails has a powerful effect on your body's electromagnetic energy. If you cut your hair or nails at the wrong time of the month, you can reduce your level of vitality significantly. Use these dates to ensure you optimise your energy levels by staying in tune with the stars.

Hair and nails

January	1, 2, 3, 4, 5, 6, 7, 8, 11, 12, 13, 14, 15, 18, 19, 20, 21, 22, 25, 26, 27
February	3, 4, 5, 7, 8, 15, 16, 17, 18, 19, 22, 23, 24, 25
March	2, 3, 4, 6, 7, 8, 14, 15, 21, 22
April	1, 2, 3, 4, 5, 10, 11, 12, 17, 18, 19, 20, 21, 22, 23, 28, 29, 30
May	1, 2, 3, 4, 5, 7, 8, 9, 10, 11, 12, 13, 15, 16, 17, 18, 25, 26 27, 28, 29, 30
June	4, 5, 11, 12, 14, 15, 16, 24, 25
July	1, 2, 3, 8, 9, 12, 13, 14, 21, 22, 28, 29, 30
August	1, 2, 5, 6, 17, 18, 19, 25, 26
September	1, 2, 6, 7, 14, 15, 21, 22, 23, 24, 28, 29, 30
October	3, 4, 11, 12, 18, 19, 20, 25, 26, 27, 28, 29, 30
November	7, 8, 9, 14, 15, 16, 22, 23, 24, 25, 26, 27
December	5, 6, 12, 13, 19, 20, 21, 22, 23, 24, 25

Therapies, massage and self-pampering

January	6, 7, 13, 14, 15, 18, 19, 20, 21
February	2, 3, 9, 11, 14
March	1, 9, 14, 16, 17, 20, 23, 29
April	4, 5, 6, 10, 11, 12, 13, 17, 25, 26
May	2, 3, 7, 8, 9, 10, 11, 14, 15, 16, 17, 22, 23, 24, 31
June	3, 5, 12, 18, 19, 26, 27
July	4, 7, 8, 9, 10, 16, 23, 28, 29, 30, 31
August	3, 4, 5, 6, 7, 13, 20, 21, 24, 25, 26, 27, 28, 31
September	2, 17, 21, 28, 29

October	13, 14, 15, 18, 19, 21, 25, 26, 27, 28
November	2, 3, 9, 11, 14, 15, 16, 17, 21, 24, 29
December	7, 12, 13, 14, 15, 18, 19, 20, 22, 26, 27, 28, 29

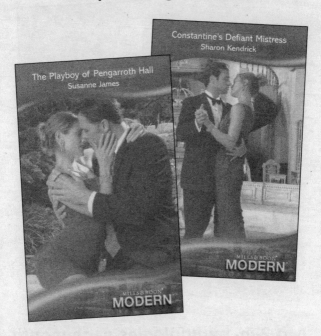

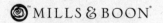

ROMANCE

Pure romance, pure emotion

Two 2-in-1 anthologies each month

Available on the first Friday of every month
from WHSmith, ASDA, Tesco, Eason
and all good bookshops
Also available as eBooks
www.millsandboon.co.uk